SPIRITUAL AUTOBIOGRAPHY

Discovering and Sharing Your Spiritual Story

A SPIRITUAL FORMATION STUDY GUIDE
BY RICHARD PEACE

D0067740

A NavPress resource published in alliance
with Tyndale House Publishers, Inc.

NAVPRESS⬤

NavPress is the publishing ministry of The Navigators, an international Christian organization and leader in personal spiritual development. NavPress is committed to helping people grow spiritually and enjoy lives of meaning and hope through personal and group resources that are biblically rooted, culturally relevant, and highly practical.

For more information, visit www.NavPress.com.

Copyright © 1998 by Richard Peace. All rights reserved.

A NavPress resource published in alliance with Tyndale House Publishers, Inc.

NAVPRESS and the NAVPRESS logo are registered trademarks of NavPress, The Navigators. Absence of ® in connection with marks of NavPress or other parties does not indicate an absence of registration of those marks.

TYNDALE is a registered trademark of Tyndale House Publishers, Inc.

ISBN 978-1-57683-110-6

Cover illustration: Wood River Media, Inc.

(Orginally published as *Spiritual Storytelling: Discovering and Sharing Your Spiritual Autobiography,* copyright © 1996 by Richard Peace, this edition has been fully revised and updated.)

Printed in the United States of America

19 18 17 16
16 15 14 13 12

CONTENTS

SPIRITUAL FORMATION STUDY GUIDES
BY RICHARD PEACE

Spiritual Journaling:
Recording Your Journey Toward God

🍃

Spiritual Autobiography:
Discovering and Sharing Your Spiritual Story

🍃

Contemplative Bible Reading:
Experiencing God Through Scripture

🍃

Meditative Prayer:
Entering God's Presence

HOW TO USE THIS GUIDE

Introduction

I first learned about the power of sharing our stories while an undergraduate at Yale. During my final year I became a member of what was called a Senior Society. They consisted of small groups of men (Yale was not yet coed) who met together regularly. The activities of each group were kept private. In our group one of the things we did was tell our life stories to one another. This was a powerful experience for me. It was a time of self-discovery and a time when I began to discover the humanity of others outside my own circle. Up to that point my friends had been drawn mainly from Yale Christian Fellowship. But now I was the only "religious" person in the group.

I came to appreciate these other men who were so different from me. Until then, I'd had a fairly strong "us/them" mentality—"us" the Christians and "them" the worldly others. I learned how diverse our stories were. I learned how everyone struggled and everyone cared. I was the "Christian" in the group, but I was not the only one with a sense of God or a desire to be good and to do right. I learned the power of telling our stories to one another: how this bound us together in our diversity. It was hard to disdain people whose stories I knew.

Many years later, when I designed a seminary course called "The Pursuit of Wholeness," I revived this idea of sharing life stories. I asked the students to organize themselves into small groups of five or six. After some preliminary sharing and group-building, each student was given one group session in which to share his or her spiritual autobiography. After each presentation, the group responded to the story. This exercise proved deeply meaningful to my students. Consistently over the years, students rated this experience near the top of what they most appreciated about the course.

This experience forms the background of *Spiritual Autobiography*. This book is the product of twenty years of teaching "The Pursuit of Wholeness." I am indebted to my students for their feedback. I have expanded the course handout that describes how to write a spiritual autobiography into pages 57-103 of this book.

5

I also have added Bible studies on Abraham. The story of his pilgrimage contains many elements of a spiritual autobiography. He had his good times when he proved himself to be a faithful and reliable friend of God. But he also had his more frequent bad times when he proved himself to be weak, fearful, inadequate, obstinate, sinful, and mean. In other words, he was no plastic saint whose perfection is forever beyond us. He struggled just as we do. And he encountered God. His story is marked by the presence of God, despite his many inadequacies. So, too, our stories. We are not called, as was Abraham, to the awesome task of founding a nation that will become the people of God. But we are called to other tasks, all part of God's work of building a kingdom. Our stories, like Abraham's story, bear the imprint of God. I hope that studying Abraham's life will help you to prepare a more perceptive rendering of your own story.

I used a number of traditional resources in preparing the Bible studies, including Bible dictionaries, an atlas, and several studies about Abraham. The most helpful resources were four commentaries:

> *Genesis* (the Interpretation series) by Walter Brueggemann. Atlanta: John Knox Press, 1982.
> *Genesis 1-15* and *Genesis 16-50* (volumes 1 and 2 in the Word Bible Commentary series) by Gordon J. Wenham. Waco, TX: Word Books, 1987, 1994.
> *Genesis 12-50* by A. S. Herbert (Torch Bible Commentaries). London: SCM Press, 1962.
> *Genesis* by Derek Kidner (Tyndale Old Testament Commentaries). Downers Grove, IL: InterVarsity, 1967.

What is this study guide all about?
This guide will equip you to write and/or tell your spiritual autobiography. Ideally, you will meet with a small group in which each person prepares a spiritual autobiography and then shares it with the group. Even if you don't have a group, writing your spiritual autobiography will help you see the patterns and direction of your own life. If you meet with a group, each person is given an entire group session to share and discuss his or her spiritual autobiography.

6

Is this guide designed for church members only?
No—anyone can use it. God is active in everyone's life whether they acknowledge it or not. By writing and/or telling their stories, people who are not consciously following God may see and understand God's activity in their lives and may respond to God in new ways. The material in the study guide is written in ordinary language for the most part. When theological terms are used, they are explained. Though this guide is written from the perspective of Christian spirituality, it is not necessary for the user to be a Christian in order to benefit from the process of exploration.[1]

What will I learn?
You will learn three things:

- ❖ how to examine your life in order to understand the ways in which God has been active there,
- ❖ how to notice the activity of God in your life and in the lives of those around you (the spiritual discipline of noticing), and
- ❖ how to share with others what God has been doing in your life and your responses to God's activity—the good, the bad, and the ugly!

How is this study guide put together?
There are three major parts to this study guide:

- ❖ *A Small Group Guide*—material that will help you form a group and study Abraham's pilgrimage. You will study Abraham's life while group members work on their spiritual autobiographies. When you are ready to shift to sharing your spiritual autobiographies, you will use the instructions for a sharing session.
- ❖ *How to Prepare a Spiritual Autobiography*—a guide to developing your spiritual autobiography.
- ❖ *Leader's Notes*—a thorough leader's guide for the person who will facilitate your group's time together.

7

Can I use this guide on my own?
Sharing your story with others is as valuable as writing it down for yourself. However, if you don't have a group, you will still benefit greatly from writing your spiritual autobiography. Pages 57-103 will walk you through that process.

How will this process benefit me?
Preparing your story causes you to notice and remember what God has been doing in your life over time. It helps you understand your story: who you are, what God has done in and through you, and where God is urging you to go in your pilgrimage. By sharing your story with others, you come to a better understanding of your uniqueness as a child of God.

How long will the small group last?
This depends upon the group. You will need at least one formation session, one concluding session, plus a number of sessions equal to the number of people in the group (each person's story takes a full session).

There are also five Bible studies on the story of Abraham. The group can use these while members are preparing their spiritual autobiographies. You can use some, all, or none of these studies, depending on how much time it takes for the first person to prepare his or her spiritual autobiography.

What kind of commitment is involved?
If you meet with a group, each person agrees to prepare and share a spiritual autobiography. Each person also agrees to abide by the Small Group Covenant, which is discussed on page 19.

Will we do Bible study?
Yes, if you wish. During the weeks when the group does these Bible studies together, individual members are preparing their spiritual autobiographies. However, it is not necessary to do the Bible studies. After the organizational meeting, you can launch right into the first spiritual autobiography if people are prepared.

How do I recruit members for a group?
All it takes to start a group is the willingness of one person to make some phone calls. When you invite people to join the group, be sure to explain how it will operate because this is a different type of small group. Lend a copy of this book if someone wants a clearer sense of what the group is all about.

What does the group leader do?
In order to derive the most benefit from this material, your group should choose someone to function as the leader. It is then important for that person to read "The Art of Leadership" (pages 106-107) and "The Structure of Each Session" (page 107). "Adapting Material for Your Group" (pages 109-110) will be helpful if you lack time to cover all of the Bible studies, the sharing of spiritual autobiographies, and the final celebration session. In addition, before each session, the leader should go over the notes for that session.

Note
1. Assigning a gender to God is problematic. The Bible generally uses masculine language (and occasionally feminine terms)—not, of course, to imply gender but to indicate personhood. An increasing number of Christians are offended by strict masculine language (knowing the God of the Bible is neither male nor female). Others are offended by gender-neutral language. I have chosen to use traditional masculine pronouns on those few occasions when the circumlocutions of gender-neutral language make the text ponderous, but I recognize that God is not male and that the English language is deficient at this point.

9

Pilgrimage

Group Note: Leader's Notes for this session can be found on page 110.

Preparation for Sharing
To write a spiritual autobiography is a sacred task in that the process makes us aware of the spiritual dimension of our lives. God is active in all lives at all times, but not all people notice — much less respond to — God. To write a spiritual autobiography is to notice, and noticing enables us to respond in new ways to God. In this session you will discuss the process of preparing a spiritual autobiography.

Bible Study Theme
Our spiritual autobiography is the story of our pilgrimage. The model for pilgrimage is Abraham. Out of his obedience, God formed the nation of Israel. From that nation all of the nations on earth were embraced. Studying Abraham's story will give you insight into the nature of pilgrimage.

Session Aims
The purpose of this first session is to begin the process of group-building by sharing some of your stories with one another. We also will discuss the process of writing a spiritual autobiography and will do a Bible study that introduces the idea of pilgrimage by looking at Abraham's pilgrimage (Hebrews 11:1-3,8-10; 12:1-2).

STORIES
                                                                    20 Minutes
At the beginning of each session you will be asked to share a mini-story: an incident from your life that connects with the theme of the session.

Biographies
The story of your life is a network of intersecting stories—the story of your family; of your community and schools; of your friends and acquaintances—and how all this, along with your own internal story, have made you who you are.

1. Introduce yourself to the group:

   a. Briefly describe one fact about yourself that others in the group might not have guessed (for example, you grow prize-winning lilies; your hobby is bass fishing; you grew up with someone who is now nationally known).

   b. Give one reason why you came to this small group.

2. Take a few minutes to identify the important people in your story:

   ❑ your parents
   ❑ your siblings
   ❑ your relatives
   ❑ your heroes/heroines
   ❑ your spouse and children
   ❑ your important friends
   ❑ your mentors

3. When were you first aware of God's entrance into your story? Tell a sentence or two about that time.

DISCUSS   15-20 Minutes
Writing a Spiritual Autobiography
Review together "The Role of a Spiritual Autobiography" (pages 57-63). Then respond to the following questions, which relate to preparing a spiritual autobiography.

4. a. As you think about writing a spiritual autobiography, what about this process excites you?

   b. What, if anything, do you find yourself resisting?

5. How will you gather data for your spiritual autobiography?

   ❏ from journals
   ❏ from parents
   ❏ from relatives
   ❏ from photo albums
   ❏ from memory
   ❏ from telephone conversations
   ❏ from reading
   ❏ from other sources:

6. What motivates you the most in this spiritual autobiography project?

   ❏ the chance to explore God's actions in my life
   ❏ the desire to be more self-aware
   ❏ the need to know the next steps God wants me to take
   ❏ the desire to track God's impact on my life
   ❏ the wish to understand the meaning of my life
   ❏ the chance to make sense of my past
   ❏ the desire to notice the presence of God
   ❏ the need to know my growing edge
   ❏ a hungry curiosity
   ❏ other:

STUDY   **20-40 Minutes**

The Christian pilgrimage is characterized by two features: movement and goal. We are persons who press on in our spiritual lives, trying not to be stalled, side-tracked, or trapped in one place. And we have a clear sense of our goal: to be conformed to the image of Christ. Faith is the energy that drives our pilgrimage forward. In chapters 11 and 12 of Hebrews, the author describes both the process (goal-oriented pilgrimage) and the energy (God-given faith) of pilgrimage. Read over these excerpts below.

¹Now faith is being sure of what we hope for and certain of what we do not see. ²This is what the ancients were commended for.

³By faith we understand that the universe was formed at God's command, so that what is seen was not made out of what was visible. . . .

⁸By faith Abraham, when called to go to a place he would later receive as his inheritance, obeyed and went, even though he did not know where he was going. ⁹By faith he made his home in the promised land like a stranger in a foreign country; he lived in tents, as did Isaac and Jacob, who were heirs with him of the same promise. ¹⁰For he was looking forward to the city with foundations, whose architect and builder is God (Hebrews 11:1-3,8-10).

¹Therefore, since we are surrounded by such a great cloud of witnesses, let us throw off everything that hinders and the sin that so easily entangles, and let us run with perseverance the race marked out for us. ²Let us fix our eyes on Jesus, the author and perfecter of our faith, who for the joy set before him endured the cross, scorning its shame, and sat down at the right hand of the throne of God (Hebrews 12:1-2).

The Function of Faith

7. a. In Hebrews 11:3, the author gives one example of how faith operates in everyday life. What is his example and how does it illustrate faith in operation?

b. How does faith function in your relationships?

c. In your spiritual life?

d. In your understanding of the future?

e. In what ways does faith energize a pilgrim's journey?

Abraham's Faith
8. a. In what ways did Abraham demonstrate his faith in God?

b. What was the nature of his movement?

c. What was his goal?

d. How did faith play a part in his life?

Pilgrimage
9. a. Abraham is one of the witnesses that the writer of Hebrews points to in chapter 12. According to chapter 12 what hinders a person's pilgrimage?

b. How ought a person conduct his or her pilgrimage?

c. In what ways is Jesus a pilgrim's example? What was the goal toward which he pressed?

Our Pilgrimage

10. a. What do you learn from this passage about movement and process?

   b. About goals and outcome?

   c. About the role of faith?

11. (Optional) Discuss the following statement: "To be a pilgrim demands a kind of holy restlessness that keeps us moving, and a kind of invigorating hope that keeps us focused."

PRAY   **5-10 Minutes**

End your time with prayer together in a manner which is appropriate to your group. Pray about:

❖ *the formation of the group*: that the people in this small group will be drawn together and begin to feel a connection with one another

❖ *the writing of spiritual autobiographies*: that each person will find the desire and the will to engage in this process; that in so doing, new insight will emerge; and that the process itself will be energizing

❖ *pilgrimage*: that each person will grow to understand the nature and meaning of their pilgrimage

❖ *openness to God*: that each person will know God in new ways

HOMEWORK

Read pages 57-78 to get an idea of how to write a spiritual autobiography. (If you have time, read all the way through page 103.) As thoughts occur to you about your spiritual journey, make notes. This will help you later when you actually put together your spiritual autobiography.

Call & Blessing

Group Note: Leader's Notes for this session can be found on page 111.

Preparing for Sharing
In order to feel comfortable sharing your life with others, you need to be clear about the character of the group. What is expected of each person? Will what you share be kept confidential? How will the group function? These questions are covered in a group covenant. A covenant makes explicit the ground rules of the group. In this session you will decide on a covenant together.

Bible Study Theme
Abraham's pilgrimage begins with a call from God to leave his country, clan, and family home and go to Canaan, an unknown land. God also blesses Abraham. We, too, need to hear God's call and receive his blessing on our pilgrimages.

Session Aims
The purpose of this second session is to continue the process of group-building by sharing more of your stories with one another. We also will commit to a covenant to guide your small group sharing and will examine Abraham's call and blessing as Abraham begins his pilgrimage to the promised land (Genesis 12:1-5).

STORIES   **20 Minutes**
Family Stories
We learn the meaning of our own story as we hear the stories of our family, community, faith tradition, and nation.

1. When is your family most likely to tell family stories?

   ❑ at holiday gatherings
   ❑ during summer vacations
   ❑ by long-distance phone calls
   ❑ at large family dinners/picnics
   ❑ when siblings get together
   ❑ at weddings, baptisms, or confirmations
   ❑ in letters
   ❑ around the campfire
   ❑ in everyday gossip
   ❑ never
   ❑ other:

2. Tell a favorite family story about one of the following:

   ❑ a family trip
   ❑ an unusual friend or relative
   ❑ a prank
   ❑ a summer vacation
   ❑ a television show or movie
   ❑ a sports event
   ❑ a habit or idiosyncrasy
   ❑ an embarrassing moment
   ❑ any other event

3. a. How did Christ enter into your family history, if at all?

   b. Who is the most religious person in your extended family? The least religious?

DISCUSS   **15-20 Minutes**
Creating a Covenant
Every small group needs a covenant (or contract) that defines
how the group will function. A covenant is a set of ground
rules that guide interaction and establish expectations. What
follows is a draft of a covenant for your spiritual autobiography
group. Adapt it by answering the following questions:

❖ Should any of the ground rules be deleted?
❖ Should any new items be added?

When you all agree, sign your covenant, then pray together
offering your covenant to God.

Small Group Covenant
❏ *Attendance*: I agree to be at the session each week unless a
  genuine emergency arises.
❏ *Participation*: I will enter enthusiastically into group discussion and sharing.
❏ *Preparation*: I will take the time to prepare a thoughtful
  spiritual autobiography.
❏ *Confidentiality*: I will not share with anyone outside the
  group the stories of those in the group.
❏ *Honesty*: I will be forthright and truthful in what is said. If I
  do not feel I can share something, I will say, "I pass," for
  that question.
❏ *Openness*: I will be candid with others in appropriate ways
  and allow others to share for themselves.
❏ *Respect*: I will not judge others, give advice, or criticize.
❏ *Care*: I will be open to the needs of others in appropriate
  ways.

Signed: _____

Also, discuss what you read for your homework. Was there
anything in the reading that seemed especially significant to
you? Do you have questions about anything you read?

STUDY   **20-40 Minutes**

Abraham is the father of the Jewish nation. As such, he is an important figure not only to Jews but also to Christians and Muslims. This makes him one of the most important men in the history of the world. What makes Abraham so important to so many people is not a sterling character (which he did not have), an outstanding intellect (which may have existed but is not mentioned), a charming personality (he could be pretty annoying), or substantial personal accomplishments (which were few, apart from his pilgrimage to the Promised Land). Abraham is remembered for his faithfulness in obeying God's call to undertake a long and demanding journey. It was not so much what Abraham did as what God did.

Abraham's pilgrimage is a model for our pilgrimages. Not that we will experience exactly what he experienced. Rather, his pilgrimage defines the ways in which God interacts with human lives. Abraham's pilgrimage contains many of the elements common to pilgrimages: success, failure, faithfulness, unfaithfulness, troubled relationships, fulfilling relationships, and so on. In other words, in Abraham we see an ordinary man through whom God works, not because of who Abraham was, but because of who God is. Abraham's story also says some important things about God: It is possible to have a relationship with God. God calls people. God works through people to accomplish God's tasks.

Paul said, "Consider Abraham" in his letter to the Galatians (3:6). In other words, "Learn from him." This is what we propose to do. In learning from Abraham we learn about ourselves—specifically, we gain insight about the anatomy of a pilgrimage. This is important because our spiritual autobiography is the story of our pilgrimage.

¹The LORD had said to Abram, "Leave your country, your people and your father's household and go to the land I will show you.

²"I will make you into a great nation
    and I will bless you;
I will make your name great,
    and you will be a blessing.

³I will bless those who bless you,
and whoever curses you I will curse;
and all peoples on earth will be blessed through you."

⁴So Abram left, as the LORD had told him; and Lot went with him. Abram was seventy-five years old when he set out from Haran. ⁵He took his wife Sarai, his nephew Lot, all the possessions they had accumulated and the people they had acquired in Haran, and they set out for the land of Canaan, and they arrived there. (Genesis 12:1-5)

Abraham's Call
4. a. What command does God give to Abraham?

  b. What price must Abraham pay in order to obey this call?

God's Promise
5. a. What does God promise Abraham directly and by implication?

  b. What does it mean to be blessed by God? To bless others?

Abraham's Obedience
6. a. What difficulties must Abraham have experienced in obeying God's call?

  b. What made it possible for him to overcome these difficulties?

Your Call

7. a. In the past, what has God called you to do or be?

   b. Now what is God asking of you?

   c. What is the price of obedience to this calling?

   d. Are there any ways you are being called to "leave home"?

Your Blessing

8. a. If to be blessed is to be affirmed and empowered for the future, who has played this role in your life, and how did they do it?

   ❑ a grandparent
   ❑ a parent
   ❑ a spouse
   ❑ a sibling
   ❑ a wise friend/counselor
   ❑ a teacher
   ❑ yourself
   ❑ no one
   ❑ other:

   b. Whom have you blessed or could you bless? What would this mean to them?

9. (Optional) Discuss the following statement: "To hear God's call assumes we have learned to hear God; to obey God's command assumes we have learned what it means to obey God."

PRAY

End your time with prayer together in a manner appropriate to your group. Pray about:

- ❖ *the formation of the group:* that you will grow to love and trust one another; that you will become the kind of friends that support one another

- ❖ *the presentation of your stories:* that each will grow and learn from the stories; that in the telling, each person will grow more certain of his or her identity in Christ

- ❖ *the covenant:* that God will use this to bind you together and to guide your deliberations

- ❖ *the call and blessing:* that each person will hear God's call and be able to respond in positive ways; that the hardships that stand in the way of obedience will be overcome; that each person will be blessed and give blessings

HOMEWORK

Finish reading pages 57-103. Also, read session 6 (pages 49-52), which describes the group process for sharing autobiographies. Then work on defining the major periods in your spiritual journey (see pages 65-71). This work will give you a time structure in which to tell your story.

Encounters

Group Note:
Leader's Notes for
this session can be
found on page 111.

Preparation for Sharing
While there is great value in writing a
spiritual autobiography, there is even
more value in sharing it. There are three
reasons for this. First, in the telling of our
story, we come to accept who we are in new ways. Second, in the
hearing of others' stories, we come to understand our own stories better. And finally, in the telling and the hearing, we are
bound together in new and deep ways. In this session you will
discuss the process of sharing spiritual autobiographies.

Bible Study Theme
Abraham has been on his pilgrimage now for some years. It has
not been easy. He has dealt with family strife, war, and famine,
and God has not yet fulfilled his promise to give Abraham an heir.
In the passage that follows, God speaks to Abraham once again,
this time in mystical ways. In our pilgrimages, the unusual, the
unexpected, or the deep encounter often sheds new light on our
paths and gives us renewed energy to continue the journey.

Session Aims
The purpose of this third session is to continue building relationships among group members. We also will discuss the
process of sharing a spiritual autobiography, create a schedule
for sharing, and study Abraham's mystical encounter with God
(Genesis 15:1-21).

STORIES   20 Minutes

Strange Happenings

God speaks to us in various ways: sometimes softly, sometimes loudly, most often indirectly. Today we will discuss the experiences of "presence" that are rare for most people, but that are deep in meaning and clearly have the sense of the divine about them.

1. In which of the following situations or environments have you experienced the presence of God (or the supernatural) in an unusual way? Check all that apply:

   ❑ a mystical experience
   ❑ a conversion experience
   ❑ a dream with deep meaning
   ❑ reading a Bible passage
   ❑ an unusual worship experience
   ❑ in nature
   ❑ in a time of prayer
   ❑ in music or art
   ❑ the still, small inner "voice"
   ❑ through an event
   ❑ in a relationship
   ❑ by means of inconsolable longing
   ❑ in conversation
   ❑ during childbirth or lovemaking
   ❑ through a "coincidence" (which is really God acting)
   ❑ in an encounter with a child or a wise person

2. Share briefly one of these experiences. (Remember that you may cover this in more detail when you present your spiritual autobiography.)

3. If you could ask God for one type of divine encounter right now, what would it be? What do you want most from God?

DISCUSS   **15-20 Minutes**
Sharing a Spiritual Autobiography
Review the plan for presenting spiritual autobiographies in session 6 (pages 49-52). By now you also have read pages 57-103 and have begun to make notes about your story. Discuss the process of presenting a spiritual autobiography.

4. As you think about presenting your story to the group:

   a. What is the most exciting aspect of this process for you?

   b. Does anything in this process frighten or confuse you? If so, what?

   c. What will help you most when it is your turn to present?

5. Together, produce a schedule for sharing spiritual autobiographies. Who will share on which date? Include in your schedule the name of the person who will lead the post-presentation discussion.

You can begin the sharing at your next meeting if someone will be ready by then. Or, if the group needs more time to prepare, you can use session 4 (and perhaps also session 5) while the first presenter is getting ready.

STUDY   20-40 Minutes

Abraham is struggling with Sarah's barrenness. God responds
with a renewed promise and a new covenant. At the heart of
this story is a complex encounter with God that has two parts
to it: a vision, then deep sleep as God's presence passes through
the sacrifice. In this story various issues are raised: the nature
of God's promises, the delay in fulfillment, and how faith and
encounters with God function in our lives. Abraham acts as
prophet, priest, and king. As with other prophets he is granted
a vision (verse 1) and a prophecy about the future (verses 13-
16). As priest he prepares and offers a sacrifice to God (verses
9-11). As king he is promised a land and victory over his foes
(verses 16,18-21).

> ¹After this, the word of the LORD came to Abram in a vision:
> "Do not be afraid, Abram.
> I am your shield,
> your very great reward."

²But Abram said, "O Sovereign LORD, what can you give me
since I remain childless and the one who will inherit my estate
is Eliezer of Damascus?" ³And Abram said, "You have given me
no children; so a servant in my household will be my heir."
⁴Then the word of the LORD came to him: "This man will
not be your heir, but a son coming from your own body will be
your heir." ⁵He took him outside and said, "Look up at the
heavens and count the stars—if indeed you can count them."
Then he said to him, "So shall your offspring be."
⁶Abram believed the LORD, and he credited it to him as
righteousness.
⁷He also said to him, "I am the LORD, who brought you out of
Ur of the Chaldeans to give you this land to take possession of it."
⁸But Abram said, "O Sovereign LORD, how can I know that I
will gain possession of it?"
⁹So the LORD said to him, "Bring me a heifer, a goat and a
ram, each three years old, along with a dove and a young
pigeon."
¹⁰Abram brought all these to him, cut them in two and
arranged the halves opposite each other; the birds, however, he

did not cut in half. ¹¹Then birds of prey came down on the carcasses, but Abram drove them away.

¹²As the sun was setting, Abram fell into a deep sleep, and a thick and dreadful darkness came over him. ¹³Then the LORD said to him, "Know for certain that your descendants will be strangers in a country not their own, and they will be enslaved and mistreated four hundred years. ¹⁴But I will punish the nation they serve as slaves, and afterward they will come out with great possessions. ¹⁵You, however, will go to your fathers in peace and be buried at a good old age. ¹⁶In the fourth generation your descendants will come back here, for the sin of the Amorites has not yet reached its full measure."

¹⁷When the sun had set and darkness had fallen, a smoking firepot with a blazing torch appeared and passed between the pieces. ¹⁸On that day the LORD made a covenant with Abram and said, "To your descendants I give this land, from the river of Egypt to the great river, the Euphrates—¹⁹the land of the Kenites, Kenizzites, Kadmonites, ²⁰Hittites, Perizzites, Rephaites, ²¹Amorites, Canaanites, Girgashites and Jebusites" (Genesis 15:1-21).

The Promise

6. a. Review the list in question 1. In how many ways does God reveal himself here to Abraham?

   b. What three promises does God give Abraham in this chapter (verses 1,4-5,18-21)?

   c. What prophecy does God give (verses 13-16)?

The Protest

7. a. What is Abraham's first protest (verses 2-3)? Why does Abraham protest?

   b. How does Abraham respond to God's word and sign?

c. What is Abraham's second protest (verse 8)?

The Response

8. a. What moved Abraham from protest in verses 2-3 to faith in verse 6?

   b. How does God respond to his second inquiry?

   c. What is the connection between faith and delay? Between faith and encounter with God?

9. It is one thing to have a mystical experience with God; it is another to live in God's presence daily. In what ways do you know God's presence in daily life?

10. It is one thing to know God's promises and presence; it is another to live with the doubts, issues, and delays that comprise the walk of faith for most people.

    a. What have been (or are) your complaints to God?

    b. What role, if any, has doubt played in your pilgrimage?

    c. How do you deal with the delays (the time gap between promise and fulfillment; between prayer and response)?

11. (Optional) Discuss the following statement: "To open ourselves to the supernatural is a tricky business. We need to

be sure it is God whom we have met, and we need to be sure that our experience is not just wishful thinking."

PRAY   **5-10 Minutes**
End your time with prayer together in a manner appropriate to your group. Pray about:

❖ *the writing of the spiritual autobiographies:* that each person will be able to do what is necessary

❖ *the sharing of the spiritual autobiographies:* that nervousness may be overcome, that it will be a powerful and positive experience for both presenter and group

❖ *the encounter with God:* that each person will understand how we meet God; that there will be openness to God's presence

❖ *the role of faith in our lives:* that each person's faith will be strengthened; that we will be able to deal with the delays, doubts, and questions raised in our pilgrimages; that it will be said of us that we believed God and it was credited to us as righteousness.

HOMEWORK
Once you have decided when your spiritual autobiography is due, develop a schedule so you will be finished in plenty of time. Start working on the phase of your story that is clearest to you. It is important to begin writing your story or making notes to guide your telling of it. Beginning is the hardest step.

Relationships

Group Note:
Leader's Notes for this session can be found on page 111.

Preparation for Sharing
By now you have begun work on your spiritual autobiographies. You will probably need encouragement from one another in this process. For some, writing a spiritual autobiography is an easy task; for others it is difficult. A few people find it an almost impossible assignment. In this session you will check in with each other about your progress and encourage each other to finish your preparation.

Bible Study Theme
It's easy to idealize Abraham. But he is far from perfect. Lest we be intimidated (believing that he is so far beyond us that he is not a model for poor, weak folk like us), the two incidents we will study underscore his fallibility. As we seek to understand our pilgrimages, we realize that our stories contain failure as well as success. Both success and failure are vital parts of our tale. We also learn that our failures often are found in our relationships.

Session Aims
The purpose of this fourth session is to report on how you are doing in preparing a spiritual autobiography. We also will reflect on the relationships in your pilgrimage and will study Abraham's relationships with various people (Genesis 16:1-6; 20:1-15).

STORIES   **20 MINUTES**

Friends and Relatives

At the heart of our lives are our friends and relatives.

1. a. When you were a child, who were the three most important people in your world?

   ❏ a grandparent
   ❏ a parent
   ❏ a sibling
   ❏ other relative (aunt, cousin, et cetera)
   ❏ a neighborhood friend
   ❏ a vacation friend
   ❏ a school friend
   ❏ a pet
   ❏ other:

   b. What was the best thing you remember about these relationships?

2. When you were a teenager, who was your best friend? Describe him or her and explain why you were such good friends.

3. Have you ever had a "spiritual friendship" — a relationship that centered on your pursuit of God? If so, describe it. If not, what do you think such a friendship would be like?

DISCUSS   15-20 MINUTES

Working on a Spiritual Autobiography

At this point most people in the group are immersed in the process of preparing their spiritual autobiographies. Use this discussion time to give progress reports.

4. Where are you in the process of preparing your spiritual autobiography?

   ❑ All done
   ❑ Almost done
   ❑ In the midst of it
   ❑ Just getting started
   ❑ I work best under pressure
   ❑ Was I supposed to be working on that?

5. What is the easiest part of the process for you? The hardest part?

   ❑ getting started
   ❑ writing it down
   ❑ remembering
   ❑ finding time
   ❑ getting information
   ❑ overcoming roadblocks
   ❑ knowing what to do
   ❑ getting motivated
   ❑ dealing with doubts and fears
   ❑ other:

6. How can the group pray for you as you work on your spiritual autobiography?

STUDY   20-40 MINUTES

It's easy to think of Abraham as a saint who lived each step of his life in pure godliness. He was the father of a great nation and is revered by the world's three major religions. He experienced the direct presence of God, not once but on several occasions, calling him to a momentous task. He believed God and so became the model for salvation; he followed God and so became the model for pilgrimage. While all of this is true, it does not fully describe Abraham. He made some huge mistakes. In fact, in Abraham we see not so much the sanctity of a saint but the graciousness of God.

We are going to look at two incidents in Abraham's life, both involving a relational triangle. In the first, Sarah decides to solve the problem of her barrenness in her own way. It doesn't work. In the second incident, Abraham deals with another problem: his fear. He is no wiser than Sarah and also gets into trouble. In these two incidents we see that pilgrimage is no panacea; we do stupid things along the way that mess up our relationships. This, too, is part of our stories. In knowing ourselves and God's work in our lives, we need to confront these missteps.

[1]Now Sarai, Abram's wife, had borne him no children. But she had an Egyptian maidservant named Hagar; [2]so she said to Abram, "The Lord has kept me from having children. Go, sleep with my maidservant; perhaps I can build a family through her."

Abram agreed to what Sarai said. [3]So after Abram had been living in Canaan ten years, Sarai his wife took her Egyptian maidservant Hagar and gave her to her husband to be his wife. [4]He slept with Hagar, and she conceived.

When she knew she was pregnant, she began to despise her mistress. [5]Then Sarai said to Abram, "You are responsible for the wrong I am suffering. I put my servant in your arms, and now that she knows she is pregnant, she despises me. May the Lord judge between you and me."

[6]"Your servant is in your hands," Abram said. "Do with her whatever you think best." Then Sarai mistreated Hagar; so she fled from her (Genesis 16:1-6).

¹Now Abraham moved on from there into the region of the Negev and lived between Kadesh and Shur. For a while he stayed in Gerar, ²and there Abraham said of his wife Sarah, "She is my sister." Then Abimelech king of Gerar sent for Sarah and took her.

³But God came to Abimelech in a dream one night and said to him, "You are as good as dead because of the woman you have taken; she is a married woman."

⁴Now Abimelech had not gone near her, so he said, "Lord, will you destroy an innocent nation? ⁵Did he not say to me, 'She is my sister,' and didn't she also say, 'he is my brother'? I have done this with a clear conscience and clean hands."

⁶Then God said to him in the dream, "Yes, I know you did this with a clear conscience, and so I have kept you from sinning against me. That is why I did not let you touch her. ⁷Now return the man's wife, for he is a prophet, and he will pray for you and you will live. But if you do not return her, you may be sure that you and all yours will die."

⁸Early the next morning Abimelech summoned all his officials, and when he told them all that had happened, they were very much afraid. ⁹Then Abimelech called Abraham in and said, "What have you done to us? How have I wronged you that you have brought such great guilt upon me and my kingdom? You have done things to me that should not be done." ¹⁰And Abimelech asked Abraham, "What was your reason for doing this?"

¹¹Abraham replied, "I said to myself, 'There is surely no fear of God in this place, and they will kill me because of my wife.' ¹²Besides, she really is my sister, the daughter of my father though not of my mother; and she became my wife. ¹³And when God had me wander from my father's household, I said to her, 'This is how you can show your love to me: Everywhere we go, say of me, "he is my brother."'"

¹⁴Then Abimelech brought sheep and cattle and male and female slaves and gave them to Abraham, and he returned Sarah his wife to him. ¹⁵And Abimelech said, "My land is before you; live wherever you like" (Genesis 20:1-15).

37

Issues

7. a. What is the problem in the first story, and how does Sarah propose to solve it?

   b. How would you assess Abraham's role in this incident?

   c. What was the outcome of this first venture? Who was hurt and how?

   d. What is the problem in the second story, and how does Abraham propose to solve it?

   e. How would you define Sarah's role in this incident?

   f. What was the outcome of this second venture? Who was hurt and how?

Relationships

8. a. Describe the attitudes displayed by each of the three main characters in the first story: Sarah, Abraham, Hagar.

   b. Describe the attitudes displayed by each of the three main characters in the second story: Sarah, Abraham, Abimelech.

Your Central Issue

9. For Abraham and Sarah, the central issue of their lives was their childlessness. So much revolved around this problem. Is there a central, defining issue in your life? If so, what is it, and how have you responded to it? Here are some options:

- ❏ a need/desire to please
- ❏ a call to love
- ❏ laziness; a lack of perseverance
- ❏ a desire to succeed
- ❏ the need always to be right
- ❏ a relationship
- ❏ addictive behavior
- ❏ desire for God
- ❏ loyalty/faithfulness
- ❏ fear
- ❏ trust
- ❏ abuse in childhood
- ❏ desire to help others
- ❏ illness
- ❏ struggle
- ❏ restlessness
- ❏ fear of death
- ❏ ambition

Your Relationships

10. a. With what aspect of these two stories do you most closely identify?

b. What has your relational history been like?

c. What are your key attitudes in relationships?

39

11. (Optional) Discuss the following observation by the scholar
    Gerhard Von Rad: "The bearer of the promise is the greatest
    enemy of the promise."

PRAY   5-10 MINUTES

End your time with prayer together in a manner appropriate to
your group. Pray about:

❖ *finishing the spiritual autobiography:* that each person will
  find the energy to do so; that the process will reveal useful information concerning each person's pilgrimage

❖ *relationships:* that we are clear about the key people in
  our relational world; that we are clear about the positive
  and negative parts of our relationships; that we grow in
  our ability to love and forgive others

❖ *issues:* that we find the central, defining issue in our lives,
  if such a thing exists for us; that we understand how this
  issue has shaped us; that we learn how to trust God in
  the midst of that issue

HOMEWORK

By this stage you know what you do and do not remember
about your spiritual journey. If you need to, consult outside
sources in order to fill in the details of your memory: journals,
or friends and relatives who were with you at crucial points
and who know your spiritual history. Continue to pray about
this project and be alert to sudden insights or memories. Don't
forget why you are writing a spiritual autobiography. This is an
exercise (a discipline, actually) that helps you learn to notice
God's presence. It is not an assignment or a project to do for
the sake of itself.

Testing

Group Note:
Leader's Notes for
this session can be
found on page 112.

Preparation for Sharing
Next week you will begin sharing your
spiritual autobiographies. The upcoming
sharing is what this small group series is
all about. In this session you will discuss
the details of how the sessions will be conducted.

Bible Study Theme
God now asks Abraham to do the hardest thing he has ever
done—give up his beloved son Isaac. This is Abraham's
supreme test. Challenges come in many sizes and many forms.
Common to all tests is that as we go through them, God wants
us to trust Him.

Session Aims
The purpose of this final preparatory session is to get ready to
share your spiritual autobiographies. We also will study the hard
moments in pilgrimage (Genesis 22:1-14).

STORIES   20 MINUTES
Challenges
We thrive on them. We avoid them. We seek them out. They
frighten us. They exhilarate us. They test us. We love them. We
hate them. Challenges are part of life.

1. If you had to pick one of the following challenging sports
   to try, which one would it be and why? Which sport would
   scare you the most? Why?

   ❑ parachuting
   ❑ scuba diving
   ❑ hang gliding
   ❑ rock climbing
   ❑ mountain biking
   ❑ sea kayaking
   ❑ ultralight flying
   ❑ bungee jumping
   ❑ white-water rafting
   ❑ solo ocean sailing

2. What is the most frightening thing you have ever done?
   Describe it to the group.

3. What is your response to challenges?

DISCUSS   15-20 MINUTES
Starting to Share Your Spiritual Autobiographies
At your next meeting, the first group member shares his or her spiritual autobiography. Go over the details of what that will be like.

Schedule
4. Make sure everyone is clear as to the schedule: who shares when, and who leads when.

Leading a Sharing Session
5. a. Make sure everyone understands the process (Opening; Presentation; Discussion; Pray). Review the outline on pages 50-52.

b. Discuss the role of the small group leader (pages 49-50).

c. Discuss the process of sharing a spiritual autobiography.

d. Discuss the role of each group member (pages 50-51).

e. Discuss the time schedule.

The Final Session
6. Look over the material on pages 53-56. Even though the final session is some time away, start to think about your final celebration together.

STUDY   20-40 MINUTES

This is the high point in the relationship between God and Abraham. It expresses the tension between testing and provision, the conflict between command and promise. This time Abraham is faithful to God. And God is faithful to Abraham. This is a hard story because it occurs in such a different context from our own.[1] We cannot even imagine child sacrifice. But Abraham lived in an environment where sacrificing a firstborn child to a god was common. Furthermore, we now know conclusively that God does not call us to kill. Abraham was only beginning to learn this lesson (the Ten Commandments had not yet been given). Read this story with all of its genuine horror, but read it also as the story of a God who is teaching significant lessons to the nations through Abraham.[2]

[1]Some time later God tested Abraham. He said to him, "Abraham!"

"Here I am," he replied.

[2]Then God said, "Take your son, your only son, Isaac, whom you love, and go to the region of Moriah. Sacrifice him there as a burnt offering on one of the mountains I will tell you about."

[3]Early the next morning Abraham got up and saddled his donkey. He took with him two of his servants and his son Isaac. When he had cut enough wood for the burnt offering, he set out for the place God had told him about. [4]On the third day Abraham looked up and saw the place in the distance. [5]He said to his servants, "Stay here with the donkey while I and the boy go over there. We will worship and then we will come back to you."

[6]Abraham took the wood for the burnt offering and placed it on his son Isaac, and he himself carried the fire and the knife. As the two of them went on together, [7]Isaac spoke up and said to his father Abraham, "Father?"

"Yes, my son?" Abraham replied.

"The fire and wood are here," Isaac said, "but where is the lamb for the burnt offering?"

[8]Abraham answered, "God himself will provide the lamb for the burnt offering, my son." And the two of them went on together.

⁹When they reached the place God had told him about, Abraham built an altar there and arranged the wood on it. He bound his son Isaac and laid him on the altar, on top of the wood. ¹⁰Then he reached out his hand and took the knife to slay his son. ¹¹But the angel of the Lord called out to him from heaven, "Abraham! Abraham!"

"Here I am," he replied.

¹²"Do not lay a hand on the boy," he said. "Do not do anything to him. Now I know that you fear God, because you have not withheld from me your son, your only son."

¹³Abraham looked up and there in a thicket he saw a ram caught by its horns. He went over and took the ram and sacrificed it as a burnt offering instead of his son. ¹⁴So Abraham called that place The LORD Will Provide. And to this day it is said, "On the mountain of the LORD it will be provided" (Genesis 22:1-14).

The Test

7. a. What, exactly, does God ask Abraham to do?

   b. How does Abraham feel about Isaac?

   c. How does Abraham respond to this command?

   d. How do you think Abraham might have resolved the conflict between God's promise (that through Isaac will come a great nation) and God's command (to sacrifice Isaac)?

   e. What is the test?

The Provision

8. a. What is the temptation for Abraham?

   b. What is God's provision?

   c. What does Abraham learn about himself from this? About God?

Your Testing

9. a. In what ways have you been tested on your pilgrimage?

   b. Which is harder for you: testing (relying on God in hard circumstances) or temptation (desiring to turn your back on God to do what you want)?

Your Provision

10. a. In what ways has God provided for you?

    b. How have you experienced the reality of 1 Corinthians 10:13: "God is faithful; he will not let you be tempted beyond what you can bear. But when you are tempted, he will also provide a way out so that you can stand up under it." Be specific if you can.

    c. In the midst of testing and provision on your journey, what have you learned about yourself? About God?

11. (Optional) Discuss the following statements by Walter Brueggemann in his commentary on Genesis:

    "[Testing] occurs only in a faith in which a single God insists upon undivided loyalty, a situation not applicable to most civil religions. Testing is unnecessary in religions of tolerance. The testing times for Israel and for all of us who are heirs of Abraham are those times when it is seductively attractive to find an easier, less demanding alternative to God."

"In a world beset by humanism, scientism, and naturalism, the claim that God alone provides is as scandalous as the claim that he tests."

PRAY   5-10 MINUTES

End your time with prayer together in a manner appropriate to your group. Pray about:

❖ *finishing the spiritual autobiographies:* that each person will find the resources to do so; that the outcome will be more than worth the effort; that the process will stimulate spiritual growth

❖ *presenting the spiritual autobiographies:* that the first presenter next week will be given special grace; that his or her spiritual autobiography will set the proper tone for all of the presentations; that we as a group will know how to respond in affirming and insightful ways

❖ *testing:* that we will be strong in the midst of trials; that we will find God faithful in what we face; that we will be given the resources we need to go through our trials

HOMEWORK

Put the finishing touches on your spiritual autobiography. You might try timing the presentation. Most people have more material than they have time to present. Edit your presentation until you get down to the root issues. And remember: you are not in competition with anyone. Your story is your story. It does not have to be the most interesting or the best told or the most creative presentation. Simply be yourself. Do your best. No one is grading you; no one is judging you. Use this opportunity to further your spiritual growth.

Notes

1. Chapter 21 tells of Isaac's birth. Finally, after years of waiting and against all the odds, Sarah becomes pregnant and Isaac is born. The promise will be fulfilled. A great nation will emerge. But in chapter 22, all this changes. God's great promise is put in peril by God's dark command.

   Why was Abraham put to such an awful test? We cannot know. Perhaps because God knew the outcome. God knew that over the years Abraham had developed such a deep and unwavering trust that he would be able both to believe the promise and follow the command. Likewise, perhaps Abraham had to undergo a radical testing because with great calling (and few have had a greater calling—to father a people through which God would bless the whole world) comes great testing. Perhaps, also, God needed to show the world he is a God of life, and that the only sacrifice God will ever ask is of himself and not us.

   Out of this experience the world learned that the God of Abraham was not like the other gods. God did not require the killing of a child. Later in Israel's history, this prohibition against killing was included in the Ten Commandments. Likewise, Abraham and Isaac's experience prepared us to understand the later sacrifice of a son: God's own Son died on a cross for the sake of all humanity (Romans 8:31-32).

2. God tested Abraham: The point of the story was not whether Isaac would be killed, but whether Abraham could stand up to this test. Testing exposes the heart. But Abraham didn't know this was a test. He had to endure this awful time, torn between his love for his son and his love for God, between his joy that God has given him an heir and his horror that his heir would die, between his faith in God's promise and his willingness to obey God's command. God used this experience to free Abraham from the assumptions of his culture—that killing a child pleased God.

   Asking a father to sacrifice his son is a horrific command if ever there was one. It is especially difficult to imagine in Abraham's case. Not only did he love Isaac deeply ("Isaac whom you love"), but Isaac was a miracle child born well beyond the childbearing years of both of his parents. Isaac was also a son of promise—the heir ("your only son") given by God, the one who would fulfill God's great promises to Abraham. Herein lies the tension. It is through Isaac that God's promises will be fulfilled (Genesis 21:12). Isaac was the very point of the pilgrimage. If Isaac died, the entire pilgrimage would have been for nothing. Abraham was called to believe and obey even though these two elements were in sharp contradiction.

   The story of Abraham and Isaac is very important to the writers of the New Testament. It prepares us to understand the death of Jesus. Whereas God would not ask Abraham to sacrifice his only son, God gives up Jesus, his only Son, to die on the cross. In Jesus we find the tension between testing and providing most clearly illustrated. Crucifixion is the ultimate test. Resurrection is the ultimate provision.

Presenting a Spiritual Autobiography

Group Note:
Leader's Notes for this session can be found on page 112.

Preparation for Sharing
Below is an outline for a typical session in which one person presents a spiritual autobiography. You will use this pattern until each person has shared his or her story.

Theme
Writing a spiritual autobiography usually brings great insight. We notice patterns in our lives that we have never seen before. We understand better who we are and where God is leading us. We are clearer about our purpose on this planet. This is good. But it is even better to share our spiritual autobiography with others. Sharing our spiritual story deepens our insight. It is as if in making our private musings public we accept who we are in a new way. Private and public selves merge into a healthy unity. Receiving feedback from friends who have heard our spiritual autobiography is affirming and insightful.

Session Aims
The purpose of a spiritual autobiography session is to focus on the story of one group member. We also will interact with that story and pray God's blessing on the person who shares.

The Role of the Small Group Leader
It is important to be clear about the roles of the two central

people in a spiritual autobiography session. The focus is, of course, on the one who presents his or her spiritual autobiography. However, there is also a small group leader whose task is to create an encouraging environment for the presentation of the spiritual autobiography. Specifically, the small group leader:

- ❖ opens the session by leading a brief time of prayer
- ❖ watches the clock so that there will be adequate time for discussion after the presentation of the spiritual autobiography
- ❖ guides the discussion after the presentation
- ❖ leads the closing prayer time

OPENING   5 MINUTES

Spend a few minutes praying together. Pray for God's guidance, a comfortable and relaxed presentation, clarity on the part of the presenter, and a good discussion, filled with affirmation and insight.

PRESENTATION   30-45 MINUTES

This is the heart of the session—the presentation of a spiritual autobiography by one group member. The role of the presenter is to:

- ❖ share a well-prepared spiritual autobiography
- ❖ be honest in accordance with the level of trust in the group
- ❖ be disciplined enough to end in time for discussion
- ❖ be open to the discussion that follows

The role of each group member is to:

- ❖ give the presenter your full attention (to listen in a focused manner is a great gift)
- ❖ be affirming in your body language (how you listen helps—or hinders—the presenter)
- ❖ not interrupt (allow space for silence)

❖ not interpret (don't explain, correct, suggest, or criticize the life of another person)

❖ listen with the following questions in mind:

a. What strikes you about this story? What is similar to your own experience? What is opposite to it? (In other words, listen to that person's story in relationship to your story, noting the similarities and differences, both of which provide points for discussion.)

b. What do you learn from the story? What new insights are there for you?

c. What are the unique and special features of the presenter? What special gifts do you see in his or her life?

d. If you made a sanctified guess, into which areas of ministry might God lead the storyteller? What might be his or her place in the work of God's kingdom?

e. What, if anything, puzzles you in this story? What would you like to understand better?

DISCUSSION   15-30 MINUTES

The most common problem in a spiritual autobiography session is the lack of time to discuss what has been presented. There are various reasons for this.

First, who can compress an entire life into thirty minutes? The presenter's challenge is to select the key issues, incidents, and insights to share and to set aside others. The hardest thing is to decide what to leave out of your story.

Second, we fear judgment. We may believe that if we use up all the time, then no one can criticize us for how we have lived. This is an unwarranted fear. For one thing, in the covenant everyone specifically agrees to "not judge others, give advice, or criticize." Also, after hearing a person's story honestly told, most of us desire not to criticize but to care.

Bad time management skills also can get in the way. We

simply forget the clock. There is so much to say. This is why the small group leader has the task of watching the clock and reminding the presenter when time is almost up. The discussion should include three aspects:

❖ *Affirmation:* When the presentation is finished, begin the discussion by going around the circle and asking each person to identify, very briefly, one element of the presentation he or she most appreciated. Continue this spirit of affirmation throughout the discussion.

❖ *Resonance:* Next, using the listening questions on page 51, discuss the story itself, including what you heard in the presentation that connects with your story. The point of the interaction is mutual sharing, mutual discovery. We learn from one another. Often others "see" for us, helping us discover what God is doing in our lives.

❖ *Response:* Near the end of the discussion, allow the presenter to respond. (He or she already may have been doing this in the course of the interaction.)

PRAY   10 MINUTES

The purpose of this time of prayer is to ask God's blessing on the person who has shared his or her story. This act of blessing is a great gift we can give one another. First, affirm. Go around the circle and allow each person to name one thing he or she has come to appreciate about the presenter. Next, spend a few moments in prayer, thanking God for the presenter and asking God to guide that person as his or her life unfolds. Finally, gather around the person and have each member lay hands lightly on the person (or someone who is touching him or her). Ask God to bless and empower him or her to be God's person and to live for God's kingdom.

There are also other ways to pray. For instance, if you feel uncomfortable laying hands on the person, join hands in a circle and pray for the presenter. Also, you can combine the time of prayer and the time of blessing for the person.

Celebration!

Group Note:
Leader's Notes for
this session can be
found on page 112.

Preparation for Celebrating
Here are suggestions for conducting a
final small group session once everyone
has shared his or her spiritual autobiography. This session provides a chance to
bring closure to your small group and an opportunity to plan
future small group activities.

Theme
Sharing spiritual autobiographies draws people together. This
kind of sharing can be intense as we confront ourselves, identify
issues we have faced and must still face, and discover or reaffirm
God's calling. But after the intensity of sharing comes the joy of
celebration.

Session Aims
The purpose of this final session is to enjoy one another. We
also will remember together the experience of preparing and
sharing a spiritual autobiography, plan for the next small group
series, or say goodbye in the context of prayer and affirmation.

CELEBRATION

There are various ways to celebrate your time together. These could include:

Food: Make it a party. You could do a potluck supper or serve fancy desserts. Maybe chips and soda fit the style of your group. It doesn't matter what you eat, but be sure to include food. Eating together is always a rich experience. Food is central to celebration.

Reminiscence: This is the time for recalling fond memories of the time you spent together. While telling your stories to one another you have created new stories.

There are different ways to reminisce. You might want to ask people to share their favorite memories from the group sessions or to talk about the most memorable meeting from their point of view. Or you could laugh together about who played which role during the sessions. You might want to discuss the high and low points of your time together. If you want to do a small group exercise, you can give "awards" to each person.

Awards: Take a few minutes and ask each person to decide which "award" goes to which person. Then focus on one person in the group and let the others give their "awards," explaining the reason for the selection. (You might want to do this in groups of four.) Possible awards include:

- ❖ The funniest spiritual autobiography
- ❖ The shortest spiritual autobiography
- ❖ The longest spiritual autobiography
- ❖ The most literate spiritual autobiography
- ❖ The spiritual autobiography that would make the best novel
- ❖ The spiritual autobiography that would make the best movie
- ❖ The honesty award
- ❖ The best listener award
- ❖ The liveliness award
- ❖ The _____ award

WHAT'S NEXT?

Discuss the next step for your small group. Here are a few possibilities to talk through as a group.

❖ *Spiritual Disciplines series:* Take a short break as a group (two weeks) and then start again and work on another spiritual discipline. There are three other books in this series (see page 4). One logical next step would be *Contemplative Bible Reading: Experiencing God Through Scripture.* In this guide you will learn a new way of Bible reading (an ancient monastic practice called *lectio divina*) and see how the great stories in Scripture shed light on your story. The other two topics in this series are spiritual journaling and meditative prayer.

❖ *Bible study:* You might want to continue to meet as a small group but switch to a Bible study. Visit your local bookstore, or call NavPress at 1-800-366-7788 for suggestions about which materials to use.

❖ *Retreat:* Go on a retreat together. This is a great way to deepen your relationship with God.

❖ *Multiply:* If this has been a meaningful experience for you, why not start other spiritual autobiography groups? Work together in teams of two and recruit new members. You and your partner can continue to work on your spiritual autobiographies so that the next time you present them they will contain even more insights.

❖ *Teach:* Instruct others in the process of spiritual autobiography in a Sunday school class or one-day seminar.

❖ *Conclude:* It may be time to bring this particular small group to a close. If you do, you might want to discuss each member's plans for spiritual growth. You might also want to schedule a reunion dinner for a few months from now. Conclude the group with prayer for each other's spiritual pilgrimages.

PRAYER & FAREWELL

End with a final prayer and commissioning service. There are various ways to do this.

❖ *Group prayer:* Join hands and spend time in prayer together, committing the whole experience and each person to God.

❖ *Testimony:* Ask each person to express one new thing God has said to him or her as a result of this spiritual autobiography small group experience. Then gather around that person, lay hands on him or her, and pray for God's blessing.

❖ *Affirmation:* Focus on one person. Allow the other group members to express briefly what they have come to appreciate in that person (such as his or her courage, honesty, ability to empathize, commitment to ministry, ability to love, practical good sense, friendliness, wisdom). Then gather around that person, lay hands on him or her, and pray for God's blessing.

❖ *Liturgy:* Prepare a final liturgy (as a group or by assigning this task to one or two people) using both the ancient prayers of the church and new prayers written for the group. Use this as the final experience together.

THE ROLE OF A
SPIRITUAL AUTOBIOGRAPHY

A spiritual autobiography is the story of God's interaction in our lives. It chronicles our pilgrimage as we seek to follow God.

The first published spiritual autobiography was written by Saint Augustine, a North African bishop, at the end of the fourth century A.D. Augustine's *Confessions* is a classic of spiritual writing that has influenced countless people through the ages. The title has the double meaning: confession as praise to God and confession of one's faults to others. In *Confessions* Augustine describes how God rescued him from his wayward life and false beliefs. He records both the high points in his interaction with God (such as his conversion and the mystical experience he shared with his mother Monica) and his low points (such as taking a mistress and later sending her away). But in all of his ups and downs, the reader detects Augustine's astonishment that God graciously rescued him from his errant ideas and self-destructive behavior.

Many other spiritual autobiographies have been written since Augustine's. In the seventeenth century, the Puritans wrote spiritual autobiographies, stimulated by their need to give a personal testimony in order to become members of the church.

Recently, spiritual autobiography has blossomed as a literary genre. Hundreds of thousands of people have read about C. S. Lewis's journey to faith in *Surprised by Joy*. They also have followed his ongoing pilgrimage in the scores of letters he wrote to correspondents around the world (in *Letters to an American Lady*, for instance).

In *Seven Storey Mountain*, Thomas Merton told of his pilgrimage from cynical intellectual to Trappist monk. Merton has helped many to understand the monastic life. Dan Wakefield, screenwriter and author, recounted his spiritual journey in *Returning*. He later wrote *The Story of Your Life: Writing a Spiritual Autobiography* to help others in this process. Spiritual autobiography has become a significant form of spiritual exploration.

Spiritual autobiography is not limited to great saints and their extraordinary deeds, nor to literary giants who can write with clarity and force. Anyone can write a spiritual autobiography. Each person has a story to tell. Every one of us could write a spiritual autobiography because God is active in each of our lives. However, persistent refusal to hear and heed the Voice reduces it to a mere whisper and relegates it to the background of many lives. And more than a few people would be surprised to hear that they have anything to write about God. Yet there are hints of the divine in all lives: long-forgotten childhood experiences of God's presence; answers to prayer that were quickly shrugged off as "coincidence"; grace in the midst of pain; moments of joy that rush in unexpectedly; responses to nature that draw us outward; deep suspicion that maybe our mechanistic explanations of the way the universe operates are not as sound as we would like them to be; encounters with powers beyond us; worship that we did not initiate and could not contain; a sense of blessing that gives us hope and direction; a knowledge that somehow we are significant in this world. God is alive and active in the universe, and when we start to notice, it is hard to stop noticing.

This is one reason why it is so useful to write a spiritual autobiography. It draws the strands of our lives together in a way that points us to their meaning; it reminds us of where true reality lies in contrast to the illusions of modern life. A spiritual autobiography encourages us to notice God, and as we notice, our lives are changed.

The process of writing a spiritual autobiography is not difficult. It takes a little time, a willingness to explore areas we have previously left unexamined, and a hungry curiosity about God. Writing a spiritual autobiography is best done in the company of others who are engaged in the same task. We motivate each other to continue with the exploration; we encourage each other when the writing slows down; and most importantly, we are there to hear the finished work because the telling of each other's tale is very important.

Spiritual Autobiography and Ordinary Autobiography

One issue you will face is how to sort out the "spiritual" dimensions of your life from all of the other dimensions. In the absolute sense, of course, this is not possible. Life does not fit into neat categories, nor does God operate only in a carefully prescribed realm. In fact, God is present in all aspects of life: in the ordinary acts of eating ("Give us this day our daily bread"), sleeping (the people in the Bible knew that God could and did speak through "night visions"), and making love (God is the one who gave us our sexual natures). God is found in events, choices, and especially relationships. It is often through the "ordinary" that we encounter the "extraordinary." Out of the mundane we forge our understanding of the spiritual. God is everywhere. So a spiritual autobiography is not easily disentangled from the rest of our story, nor is it intended to be.

After having said this, I also need to say that there is a spiritual dimension to life and that it is possible to identify it. What distinguishes a spiritual autobiography from an ordinary autobiography is the lens through which we look at our lives. In this case, we view our lives through the lens of the spiritual by searching for God's footprints. We focus on aspects that reveal the activity of God.

A traditional autobiography tells the story of a life in sequential order, including all of the "facts" that make that story unique. But the writer must select some information to include and some to leave out. Who could possibly record a whole life? Who could possibly read such an account? No, a tale is told for a reason: to justify a life; to track the development of genius; to account for a life lived for good or ill; to boast; to explain; to understand. A spiritual autobiography, on the other hand, is told in order to see the activity of God.

But here is the rub. Most of the time we don't notice the spiritual. God is like the air we breathe. We merely assume God, just as we assume air. So the challenge in a spiritual autobiography is to notice God. We dare not simply say, "God is everywhere" (which is true) and then claim, "So what more can I say?" (which is a cop-out). We must start by identifying those seminal points when we have been aware of God. These may be major events (the birth of a child, a wedding, a funeral, a conversion) or hints of transcendence (the joy of a sunset, being moved by music or poetry, being struck by a passage of Scripture that helps make sense out of a problem).

To write a spiritual autobiography is to learn a new way of seeing. It is to bridge the gap between the natural and the spiritual. It is to become newly sensitive to the hidden work of God. It is to live simultaneously in the two worlds we were created to inhabit—the spiritual and the physical—and in the process to become a whole person. This is why writing a spiritual autobiography can be called a spiritual discipline: it teaches us a new way of seeing, a way of seeing God.

Spiritual Autobiography and Witness

Your spiritual autobiography is not the same as the story of your first encounter with Jesus. In some religious circles, the giving of witness often has been restricted to sharing the story of one's conversion. Now to be sure, conversion is a central element in our tale. But it is not the only element. We also need to notice and describe the many ways in which we encountered God both prior to and after conversion. To hear some people speak, it is almost as if the only important event in their spiritual lives is conversion. This is a distortion of the New Testament understanding, in which conversion marks a turning from one way to a new Way. Conversion is the beginning of a crucial new phase of spiritual experience; it is neither the beginning nor the end of the story.

Likewise, to reduce the concept of witness to sharing the story of your conversion is to limit it. How often does the opportunity present itself to take five or ten minutes to describe your conversion? Not very often; consequently evangelism training often consists of learning how to manipulate a situation so that you can "give a testimony." The result in real life can feel unnatural, awkward, and embarrassing for the one who receives such witness. The impact is frequently minimal or negative.

How much better is witness when it arises spontaneously in the context of an ongoing conversation! If we know about the many and varied ways we meet God, we have much—not simply one thing—to say. In the end, true witness is simply being honest about our ongoing experience of God.

If we are not in touch with the activity of God in our lives, we cannot talk about it. This is why writing a spiritual autobiography can be such a powerful aid in discussing our faith with those around us. The more we notice God's activity in our lives, the more we have many little stories that we can relate in the course of ordinary conversation. Such stories are less likely to intimidate our hearers. They whet a person's appetite to explore his or her own life for the presence of God. They raise the right kind of questions: "How can I know God? How can I stay connected to God? What is prayer? Where can I learn about who God is?"

Try telling a friend at work that you are in the process of trying to write a spiritual autobiography. I suspect that you will get into a good conversation about faith issues—which is what witness is all about.

Spiritual Autobiography and Growth

Perhaps the main reason we write a spiritual autobiography is so that we will grow as followers of Christ. This happens in several ways. First, we develop the skill of noticing God at work. Second, by seeing our stories as a whole we understand at a new level God's intention for us. All of the people of God have a role to play in the kingdom of God, though each role is different. Sometimes we can understand our particular role only when we see our lives in their overall context. We see how the pieces fit together. We discern how seemingly unrelated elements combine to prepare us for our various works.

Third, we grow by seeing that God has, indeed, been present and active in our lives. The security of God's presence and the encouragement of knowing we have a purpose energize us to serve God in our unique ways.

Finally, we gain some sense of the direction our lives are pointing. In understanding the meaning of our past, we understand better the meaning of the present, and we glimpse something of what the future might hold. Knowing our past helps us in our decisions about the future. Sensing the meaning of our lives, we can make the choices that are consistent with that meaning.

Sources of Data for a Spiritual Autobiography

Where do you go to find the information necessary to write a spiritual autobiography? I want to suggest several sources.

Memory: Some people only have to ask the right question in order to unlock deep memories. Simply by asking, "Where was God when I was a child (teenager, college student, parent and so on)?" brings to mind all kinds of incidents. I suggest that you begin at this point. Once you have outlined the major periods of your life, explore each period in the ways recommended in "The Content of a Spiritual Autobiography" (pages 65-78). Begin with the period that is most alive and vivid to you. Try to recall what it was like. Take notes. Be alert to thoughts that strike you or incidents that you suddenly recall. Work through each of the periods in your life in this way.

Conversation: Significant events in your spiritual life may have taken place in the presence of others. Or you may have recounted an event to friends or family members. Sometimes they have a better recollection of what went on than you. Or they may recall details that you have forgotten. It is certainly worth some phone calls to see if this is the case.

Every family has its historian. Historians may not know that this is their role, but they know more than anyone else about the history of the family. They remember what happened, who is related to whom, why one cousin no longer talks to another, who was at a family wedding twenty years ago, what the religious history of the family is, where the family skeletons are locked away, and so on. You may need to talk to the historian in your family. Again, it is worth a phone call or a lunch. This person will love to help.

Journals: One of the other books in this study guide series, *Spiritual Journaling*, describes several methods for assembling data in order to write a spiritual autobiography. The Puritans kept journals, which they considered the daily record of their sacred journey. From those journals they came to understand the story of their pilgrimage. If you have kept a journal for any length of time, reading it is the best way to get material for a spiritual autobiography.

Keeping a journal is one thing; writing a spiritual autobiography is another. In the simplest terms, a journal is the raw data from which a spiritual autobiography can be constructed. In a journal we write down the pieces of our lives: the everyday events and feelings; our reflections and impressions about life as it unfolds. Journals are of special value in writing a spiritual autobiography when we use them to assess and understand past periods of our lives.[1] We process our history through a grid that includes our key relationships, principal activities, important ideas, physical experiences, and spiritual encounters.

Prayer: In the end it is the Holy Spirit who reveals what we need to know in order to piece together a spiritual autobiography. We need to be clear about this and pray for light. We ask the Spirit to show us what we need to know about our lives in order to understand them from a spiritual point of view.

Then we listen. The Holy Spirit will lead us in various ways. Sometimes it is through our memory. If an incident pops into our heads, we do not dismiss it quickly. We think about it and write it down. At other times the Spirit speaks through our awareness and observation. After asking for guidance, we are alert to guidance: a chance remark by a friend, a phrase in a book, an incident in a television show, a story in the Bible, a prayer we are reading, a dream — whatever sparks a new line of inquiry.

Note
1. See *Spiritual Journaling: Recording Your Journey Toward God* by Richard Peace (NavPress, 1998), in which a method of journaling is described that helps people assess their past.

The Content of a Spiritual Autobiography

What, specifically, does a person write about in a spiritual autobiography? How is a spiritual autobiography organized? What is the process by which a person discerns the key issues that make up a spiritual autobiography? This chapter contains a three-step outline of the process. Use it to guide your preparation. However, remember that the important thing is not that you have followed someone else's instructions, but that *you describe your own life in a way that reflects who you are in relationship to God.*

STEP ONE: DIVIDE YOUR LIFE INTO PERIODS

Each person's life can be divided into a series of interconnecting periods of time. The advantage of dividing a life into periods is that it is much easier to work with a time frame of a few years than with an entire life of many years. Furthermore, if you do the dividing right, each period will have a theme to it; it will have an inner consistency that ties it together in some way. There are two ways to divide your life: periods based on age and periods that reflect your search for God.

Age-Based Periods

The first way to divide your life is to think of it in terms of the various stages we all go through as we grow up. These developmental periods have different characteristics.

> *Childhood:* From birth to the onset of adolescence, a person is dependent upon her parents and finds her identity primarily as a member of a family and not as an individual. Childhood is meant to be a tranquil, carefree time in which we are open to God in many different ways. Unfortunately, childhood often is filled with stress and pain, which a person must eventually deal with, often as part of a spiritual pilgrimage.

> *Adolescence:* Adolescence is a product of both physical and psychological factors. The adolescent's goal is to break free

from his family and establish an independent identity. This task often involves great turmoil. Adolescence is frequently a time of openness to God. More conversions occur during this period of life than any other.

Adulthood: This is the rest of life! Adulthood, too, has its stages:

- ❖ *Young adulthood*, when the task is to be educated or trained, find a job, leave home, and start one's own life.

- ❖ *The thirties* are typically spent raising a family and developing a career.

- ❖ *Mid-life* brings a sharp change from an external focus (on making a place in the world) to an internal focus (finding purpose and meaning) and is sometimes marked by crisis. The questions raised during this period are often spiritual.

- ❖ *The fifties* ought to be the time to enjoy the fruit of your labor while you give more time to help others. This giving reflects one's spiritual commitments.

- ❖ *Retirement* is marked by more freedom but less energy to enjoy that freedom. This is a time of summary, of drawing together the meaning of a life and expressing it in creative ways that reflect the wisdom gained through the pilgrimage.

Sub-Periods

It may be useful for you to divide these three major periods into subdivisions. For example, suppose that during your childhood you lived in two places: New York City and Cooperstown, N.Y. During the first part of your childhood your family lived in Manhattan, where your parents worked in advertising. But when you were eight they quit their jobs and bought a country inn outside Cooperstown, where they catered to a steady stream of visitors to the Baseball Hall of Fame. The first half of your childhood was spent in an urban environment and the second half in a rural one. Each period would have its own characteristics and, therefore, should be considered separately.

Sometimes the phases in our lives have more to do with people than with places. Here is another hypothetical example. At first, the central people in your life were your parents. But then your dad died and you went to live with your grandmother. Your grandmother became the most important person in your life until you made friends with a group of kids in the neighborhood, who became the center of your relational life. In this case, there would be three sub-periods during childhood revolving around parents, grandmother, and friends.

You can make the same kind of sub-divisions within each period. Locate these sub-divisions by looking for themes within a period. The two examples above concern places (moving from one location or environment to another) and people (centering your relational life around a new person or group of people). In addition to places and relationships you might look for new educational experiences (going to graduate school or taking a painting class), new groups (joining the Army or getting involved in Young Life), and new ideas (becoming a hippie or an atheist) as ways of understanding different periods.

Another way of thinking about sub-divisions in your life is to look for boundary events. A boundary event is something that launches you into a new phase of life. You may only realize that this has happened after the fact. Examples of boundary events are: marriage, the birth of child, an accident, a new job or a new place to live, college, military service, a new relationship, and starting work on a book or some other creative project.

It is perhaps most important of all to divide your adult life into its various phases. How many divisions you have will depend upon your age. If you are in your fifties when you do your spiritual autobiography, you have more periods to look back on than if you are in your twenties.

Determine the sub-divisions that make the most sense out of your life. Divide your life into a series of periods (each with some organizing theme) that are short enough to be explored with ease, but long enough to have rich content. Eight to twelve time periods work best.[1]

Search-Based Periods

There is a second way to divide your life, one that makes particular sense when writing a spiritual autobiography. You can think of your life as different periods that represent the various phases of your search for God. In this case, you would tell your story by discussing how you looked for God, how you gave yourself to God, and how you now follow God. There are three periods that typically characterize the search for God.

- ❖ *Quest:* when you sought to know God
- ❖ *Commitment:* when you came to know God
- ❖ *Incorporation:* when you live out your commitment to God

This is not to say that each person goes through each of these phases. The three phases are typical, not definitive. The search for God goes on in so many different ways it would be foolhardy to suggest that everyone follows this pattern. Furthermore, the time period for any of these phases varies greatly. For some people, neither Quest nor Commitment describes what they experience. If they grew up in church and always believed in God, their only phase is Incorporation. For others, this three-part model is concentrated on Quest. It took years to find God. They have only recently come to know God. For still others, their central problem was commitment. They knew about God; they were convinced of God's reality, but they ran from God for years. It was only gradually that they were drawn into commitment to God.

> *The Quest Phase:* The foundational question in the Quest phase is, what direction is your life pointed? Is it pointed toward God or away from God? The shift from one direction to the other, whether gradual or sudden, is worth noting in your spiritual autobiography.
>
> There are several typical "stopping places" in the quest to know God. Some of these places have names, others do not:
>
> - ❖ Believing that there is no God (atheist)
> - ❖ Wondering if God exists or not (agnostic)

- ❖ Functioning as if God doesn't exist and isn't involved
- ❖ Believing that God exists but that God is an impersonal Force, not a personal Being (deist)
- ❖ Believing in God but paying little attention to him
- ❖ Actively seeking God
- ❖ Actively fleeing God
- ❖ Actively seeking evil

The important thing is not the name you give to the various stops in the Quest to know God. It is to describe the nature of your search for God. What started you on this search? Who or what aided you? Who or what slowed your search? What kept you moving? What were the key events in your quest? Key people? Key insights? Key experiences?

The Commitment Phase: America is a religious nation, second only to India in its religious practices (according to the Gallup organization). It seems that almost everyone in the United States believes in God. However, the polls also indicate that this belief does not go very deep. The typical American who claims to believe in God does not know much about religion, nor does his or her lifestyle reflect many (if any) significant differences from the lifestyle of a similar person who does not claim to believe in God (apart, perhaps, from attending a church or synagogue). Therefore, the issue of commitment is a real one. It often marks the beginning of a new phase of spiritual life.

Commitment is not a single event, nor does it necessarily happen all at once. Commitment comes in various ways and degrees. For example, for many people their conscious spiritual life begins with commitment to the ideas of Christianity. This involves commitment to a certain view of reality, such as,

- ❖ It is not good to lie, cheat, or steal.
- ❖ Fidelity in marriage is the ideal.
- ❖ Heaven exists.
- ❖ Jesus is an inspired religious teacher whose teachings are true.

These are a few of the concepts that characterize Christianity. Different people will have different beliefs. And they will hold these beliefs with differing degrees of conviction. But believing certain things to be true and living out these beliefs are two different things. For some people, the next step in commitment is to translate their beliefs into action. Thus, for example, they do not simply say lying is wrong; they begin consciously to tell the truth in their business dealings. They have moved in their commitment from belief to action.

Another form of commitment is commitment to the church. It is not so much a matter of joining an organization as it is a commitment to a community of people. For some, commitment to the community precedes commitment to Jesus; for others, the two commitments are reversed. In either case, the nature of commitment has broadened from the individual to the community.

Perhaps the most dramatic form of commitment is conversion, whereby a man or woman enters into a conscious relationship of trust and obedience to Jesus. Conversions may be dramatic (like that of the apostle Paul or Saint Augustine) or quiet or gradual (like most people's), but they all have in common a new awareness of Jesus and a new attempt to follow him. Commitment to Jesus includes all of the previous commitments: commitment to the ideas of Christianity, to a lifestyle based on Jesus' teaching, and to the company of God's people. In fact, it generally involves a deepening of each of these previous commitments. Commitment to Jesus generally marks the dividing line between the Commitment Phase and the Incorporation Phase.

The Incorporation Phase: We never move beyond this phase. We spend our entire lives learning to be consistent disciples of Jesus. No one ever gets it fully right. In fact, people whom we would label "saints" are often the first to maintain that they are, in fact, mere novices when it comes to knowing and serving God. So, the Incorporation Phase has, of necessity, various aspects to it. Most of us should view this phase of our pilgrimage as a series of sub-periods.

These include:

- ❖ Wrestling with ideas
- ❖ Seeking to live consistently
- ❖ Finding our calling
- ❖ Learning to love
- ❖ Developing spiritual intuitions
- ❖ Moving toward community

STEP TWO: EXAMINE EACH PERIOD

Once you have divided your life into periods that make sense for you, review each period and look for material related to your spiritual autobiography. I suggest that you look for at least three things:

- ❖ Encounters with God
- ❖ Crises of Faith
- ❖ Outcomes of Growth

Encounters with God

A central feature of any spiritual autobiography is an account of instances in which the presence of God was especially vivid and/or challenging. These encounters come in various forms.

Mystical experiences: These can be overwhelming or gentle, but each has the clear sense that God is present.

Conversion experiences: In a mystical experience we encounter the living God; in a conversion experience we respond to God in repentance and faith in Jesus. Conversion occurs in different ways in different lives. For some it is quick and dramatic; for others it unfolds over time. In either case there is a conscious sense of having opened oneself to Jesus in faith.

Charismatic experiences: The work of the Holy Spirit is present in healing, by empowering, or in the fruits of the Spirit (love, joy, peace, patience, and so on).

Daily experiences: One notices God in the everyday flow of life.

The central question you must wrestle with is this: How has God made himself known to me in each period of my life? This awareness will be distinct at different times of life. In childhood, for example, God often is assumed. God just *is.* In adolescence, God often is encountered in the midst of the struggles to know oneself, so he is known through dramatic encounter. As adults, we meet God in various ways: as we experience love from another person; in discovering God's handiwork in the world around us; in the struggle to find meaning. Reflect on all of the ways in which you have encountered God.

Crises of Faith

We grow through crises. We may not like crises (I certainly don't), but a crisis often stimulates growth. Quite apart from anything else, crises force us to rely upon God. We may know it to be true in a general sense that without God we cannot cope, but mostly we muddle along until something throws us off balance and we have no choice but to reach out to God. Therefore, a good way to learn about your spiritual pilgrimage is to identify points of crisis and then to look for God's presence at those points.

There are at least five types of crises to consider in writing your spiritual autobiography:

- ❖ crisis of doubt
- ❖ crisis of circumstances
- ❖ crisis of disobedience
- ❖ crisis of depression
- ❖ crisis of darkness

Crisis of doubt: When you have faith, you have doubt. It is that simple. If everything were cut and dried, then faith would not be required, only information. But spiritual issues touch on many matters that are filled with mystery. Who would want to follow a way of life that failed to deal with mystery? Yet where there is mystery, there are questions.

In your pilgrimage you may have encountered questions that engaged you in various ways (ranging from mild curiosity to deep distress). Typical questions relate to such matters as:

- ❖ the existence of God
- ❖ the problem of evil
- ❖ the reliability of Scripture
- ❖ the historicity of Jesus' resurrection

Doubt must be faced and dealt with or it diminishes us. We need to confront questions that trouble us and we need to seek answers to these questions. Fortunately, few of our questions are new or unique. Many people have asked them over the centuries. This does not diminish the pain or power of these questions in our lives, but it does mean there are answers because some of the world's best minds have reflected a great deal on hard issues. We need to avail ourselves of this treasury of wisdom.

What questions troubled you, and how did you deal with them? In what ways did you grow as a result? How was your pilgrimage affected by these questions? In fact, doubt of one sort or another may trouble you at this moment. How will you deal with it?

Crisis of circumstances: Life does not always go smoothly. We wish it did. We try to make it so. We seek to control events so we can keep hard times at bay. Or we hide and pretend that all is well. But, in fact, issues will arise:

- ❖ a parent dies
- ❖ a relationship turns sour
- ❖ we are laid off
- ❖ illness strikes
- ❖ a tornado blows through our town

The list is endless. The question is, how do we cope? Often it is our faith that helps us to make it through. The hope at the core of the Christian message makes it possible for us to face what life sends us.

But not always. Sometimes circumstances create a crisis of faith. Our prayers seem to be ignored. We are treated unjustly and there is nothing we can do. Our parents divorce and life is not the same again. We lose hope and are unable to cope without it.

Consider some of the hard circumstances in your life. Look at the spiritual results. In what ways did you grow (or regress)? How did you cope? How could you have coped? What did you learn about God?

Crisis of disobedience: Sometimes a crisis is of our own making. We veer off in a wrong direction, and there is a price to pay. This is not to say that if we always do the right thing (as we understand it), we will automatically receive the good thing (that we want). In fact, sometimes we must suffer for doing right. We live in a universe of consequences.

Yet in our disobedience we can grow to know God in new ways—if we deal with the issue. We experience forgiveness. We learn hard lessons that protect us and make us more loving in the future. When and how did you fail? What happened? What were the results? Where was God?

Crisis of depression: Some challenges are purely emotional. Consider depression. When we are depressed, nothing else matters. We drag ourselves through life. We are unmotivated. We are sad. We can feel ourselves in decline. And we seem so powerless. We can't even pray, although we know that we need to pray. God seems remote.

There are answers to negative emotions: therapy that uncovers root causes; healing of memories that relieves pain we hardly knew existed; drugs that restore our chemical balance; loving care from others that brings us gently back to life.

What did you learn about yourself, others, and God in the midst of your emotional turmoil?

Crisis of darkness: For want of a better term, I use "darkness" to refer to those issues in our lives that have the mark of evil on them. There are various terms for this: spiritual warfare, possession, evil. The fact is that we will, on occasion, encounter individuals or systems that have a disproportionatelly negative power. In such encounters we are reminded that the apostle Paul tells us we wrestle not against flesh and blood but against principalities and powers (Ephesians 6:12). When we encounter this sort of evil, the temptation is to despair, capitulate, compromise, or surrender. The fact is, we cannot fight these battles on our own. We need prayer. We need the faith and support of others. We need the presence of Jesus.

We often grow in faith from encounters like this. In a curious way, we learn more about the supernatural aspect of life when we confront these dark elements and forces. They are a negative witness to truth.

We must be very careful, however, when we speak about encounters with darkness. There is a very real danger of attribution—pointing our fingers at others and calling them evil when, in fact, they are simply motivated by their lower natures. Be very wary of offering "the Devil made me do it" as an explanation for behavior. Still, to ignore this category is to fail to notice important facets of a spiritual pilgrimage.

Outcomes of Growth
In each period, in each event, try to notice where God was. This is not always easy. Suffice it to say that God uses all of the events and circumstances of your life to shape you into the kind of person he wants you to be. This is not always easy. We do not always cooperate with God. In fact, you may find that your pattern is to be dragged by God kicking and screaming into new growth. Nor will your story be one of unrelenting growth. You have ups and downs—these too are part of your spiritual pilgrimage.

Let me suggest various types of growth. These can be used as a grid to reflect on what you have learned in the periods of your life. These will help define the results of your story. Under each category I have listed a series of questions that you can use to assess results in each time frame. Some of these questions will not relate to you. Use what is helpful; discard what is irrelevant.

Intellectual growth: What we think shapes who we are. How we think is a product of background, environment, education, family, culture, and economics. Our aim, however, is to develop a Christ-centered worldview—one derived primarily from Scripture, not culture. Achieving this end is not easy, nor is it ever complete. Our minds grow constantly. We hope our minds will grow in the direction of truth. To this end, we need to be aware of both what we think and how we think. In addition, we need to know who and what has influenced our worldview. In this way we can say "Yes" and "No" to a particular worldview. Therefore, an important question in your spiritual autobiography will concern the state of your worldview in each period of your life.

How has your thinking about reality developed over time? What are the key ideas that shape the way you process experiences? What are the foundational facts upon which your intellectual life rests? What truths would you die for? How do you grow your mind? Who are the people who have influenced what and how you think? What are the core truths that your life is built on? In particular, what are the key theological ideas that give shape to your life?

Emotional growth: What we feel shapes us as much as what we think. We need to develop a sense of our emotional experience. The ability to access the emotional side of life varies from person to person, from women to men. In the United States, women are generally more in touch with this side than men.

What is the emotional tone of each period in your life? In particular, how did you feel about God? What did you feel about how you were living, where you were going in life, and what you were doing with your life? The emotional side expresses itself most clearly in our relationships. How would you characterize your relationships in each period of time? How would you describe your emotional life now?

Behavioral growth: Our actions reflect what we think and feel. They are the product of internal motivations. What was your behavior like in each period of time? How did the way you were living affect the spiritual side of your life? How was your behavior determined (or not) by your commitment to Christ? What behavior helped your spiritual growth; what slowed that growth?

There is often a gap between our thoughts and feelings, and the way we act in public. This is because we learn what is expected of us and we comply with those expectations, regardless of what we might think or feel. In this case, the important data will come from our private — not our public — lives. What is the nature of that gap and how are you dealing with it?

Relational growth: At the heart of our religious life is a series of relationships. Identify the key relationships in each period and how they have influenced your spiritual identity. Some relationships draw us to God; others pull us away from God. In some relationships we are the ones who give; in others we receive. In healthy relationships there is both giving and receiving. What (and how) have you learned about loving God, loving others, and loving yourself properly?

Growth in service: A key aspect of the Christian life is reaching out to others in love and service. The Bible calls us to be committed to the needs of others, especially the poor and powerless. While each person is expected to engage in general acts of charity, we also are called to specific acts of service. In your spiritual pilgrimage, how have you served both inside and outside the community of God's people?

STEP THREE: DESCRIBE EACH PERIOD

Now we come to the actual writing of your spiritual autobiography. In fact, you may have already produced your spiritual autobiography through the process of making notes in the previous two steps. Simply review your notes; identify the key incidents that tell your story; decide on the order in which to tell them; determine where you are now in your spiritual pilgrimage; and you are done!

On the other hand, you may need to work on identifying, selecting, and organizing the material. This is the subject of the next chapter. A spiritual autobiography is the story of where God was in each period in your life; how you responded (or failed to respond); and what you became out of all of this. At the heart of your spiritual autobiography will be your stories: the incidents from your life that describe where you have come from spiritually, where you are now, and where God is leading you. It is an exciting story and you will grow by discovering it.

One final note: In telling your story, keep your focus on the role of God in your life. It is easy to get side-tracked and concentrate on secondary issues of a religious or personal nature. Read through what you have written about each period and ask the question: "Where is God in my life during this period?" If the answer to this question is clear, then you have produced a spiritual autobiography.

Note

1. These seemingly arbitrary numbers come from Ira Progoff and his experience with what he calls a Steppingstone Exercise (see *At a Journal Workshop,* New York, NY: Dialogue House, 1975). Eight to twelve time periods work best in assessing a life. Too many periods cause us to lose sight of the meaning of the whole, while too few result in periods that are too long to properly assess.

THE PROCESS OF WRITING A SPIRITUAL AUTOBIOGRAPHY

The previous chapter dealt with what to say in your spiritual autobiography. This chapter addresses how to say it.

Making Notes

As you ponder the question that underlies a spiritual autobiography — *Where are the footprints of God in my life?* — you will be struck with certain thoughts, impressions, or insights. Write these down before you lose them. Not only will you preserve these impressions, you will discover new insights in the act of writing.

It might be helpful to discuss these insights with a friend. Some people gain clarity through conversation. Or you might want to do some reading. The ideas and experiences of others can clarify your own situation. For example, you remember an especially poignant time in your life. You were sitting in church listening to "Ode to Joy". You found yourself transported into a kind of ecstasy. Tears came. Then this "feeling" (though it was more than mere feeling) ended as quickly as it began, and you were left with only the longing to be back in that moment. What is the meaning of this experience? This is the sort of experience that C. S. Lewis identified as "the inconsolable longing." Look for his books. Read *Surprised by Joy* and the sermon called, "The Inconsolable Longing." You will understand better what came upon you and what it means. Do research. The more you know about the spiritual experiences of others, the better you will understand your own experience.

The Form of Your Spiritual Autobiography

Different people will create different kinds of manuscripts.

> *A complete, edited manuscript:* You may decide to write down your entire story. This might involve the production of several drafts so that the end product could be published as an article. It takes a certain facility with words and a talent for writing to do this. When you present your story to your group (if you are meeting with a group) you may

decide to read it aloud, or you may use the written version as a guide in telling it.

Notes: This is the other extreme: a series of notes, in sequence, to guide the telling of your story. This is what a gifted storyteller will often do. For example, Garrison Keillor, who for years has told "Tales from Lake Wobegon" on his weekly radio program, simply makes notes. When he stands before the microphone he lets the tale tell itself. Using this form for your spiritual autobiography means that you are comfortable with the spoken word.

A combination of notes and text: Many people find it's easier to write a fairly complete manuscript without paying much attention to grammar and spelling, and then use the manuscript to make full notes for telling the story to the group.

I would suggest that you start by trying to write a complete manuscript. If this proves too cumbersome or demanding, shift to a note format. But try your hand at writing. You may be surprised by the results. After all, what are you better qualified to write about than your own story?

Organizing Your Story

Most people tell their stories in chronological order; they skip over less important periods and focus more attention on critical events, people, and experiences. However, there are other ways to tell your tale.

Thematically: Perhaps you discover that there is a thread or theme that describes who you are and what you have experienced. Examples of themes include rescue (being lost and being found, not once but many times); grace (amazing experiences of God's work and presence in a variety of situations); travel (in all of the places where you have lived something decisive has happened that shaped your knowledge of God); relationships (yours is a story of crucial relationships: good, bad, and indifferent); addiction (entering into addictive behavior; noting, naming, and beginning to deal with it; or a life in which a single temptation has been key). Tell your story by sharing a series of vignettes that illustrate how this theme is woven through your life.

If a thematic organization appeals to you, remember that it is generally harder to communicate in this fashion than in a straightforward chronological sequence. We are used to thinking in terms of events that follow one after the other. It takes much more work to uncover a central theme and then illustrate it, but do not hesitate to try.

Metaphorically: Rather than a theme, there might be a metaphor that captures the essence of your story of interacting with God. The story of the prodigal son is one such account. You could use each of the sections in that powerful parable to describe a different phase of your story. Or perhaps the pilgrimage of Abraham describes your experience.

Through the eyes of another: It may be easier to write in the third person. Tell your story from your mother's eyes or from the point of view of your guardian angel.

As a fairy tale: "Once upon a time . . ." is the way fairy tales begin. Maybe your life is best told in this fashion.

Editing Your Story

The reason we edit our stories is not because they contain embarrassing incidents that need to be eliminated. We edit our stories because we have limited time in which to share them with others, and we cannot fit in all the stories we want to tell. It is just not possible to condense a life into thirty to forty-five minutes. (Of course, if you are writing a spiritual autobiography for your own use and not to share with a group, write as much as you like!) The challenge is to know which stories to omit and which to keep.

Once you complete your manuscript or set of notes, go back over it and read it aloud. Time yourself. If you have too much material, make some decisions on how to shorten the story even more.

Delete entire sections: This is difficult, but you may find you have two stories that deal with the same issue. If so, one can be omitted. Or you may have to select stories in order of importance, leaving out the less important ones so that the really good ones are told.

Shorten stories: Rather than cutting out whole stories, you may be able to reduce the length of several stories so that each can be told. Some of Jesus' parables demonstrate this point. Though brief, who can deny the profound meaning conveyed in the story of the good Samaritan or the prodigal son? However, be careful not to compress a story so much that you lose the heart of it. The power of a story also can be found in the details. In that case, a summary does not work as well as the full story.

Combine stories: You may be able to connect two stories into a single story, letting each illustrate the common point (rather than making the point through both stories).

In all of this, remember that sometimes "less is more." The truth of a story is, at times, more apparent when it has been cut to its bare essentials.

Creative Ways to Tell Your Story

There are other ways to tell your story than reading a manuscript or using notes. For example, if you are an artist, why not make a series of line drawings that illustrates key incidents in your spiritual autobiography? Then describe to the group what each drawing represents. Or you could raid your family photo albums and create a collage of your life from a spiritual point of view. Adding visual elements to your story will enhance it.

You might want to add an audio element—anything from segments of songs that were meaningful at different points in your life to the creation of "The Ballad of My Life," which you sing to the group.

You could redesign your spiritual autobiography as a parable, an epic poem, or a mystery tale. Don't be limited by the genre of biography. On the other hand, don't be so obscure or fictional that the group has difficulty discovering the real you.

The important thing is to make sure that what you do is appropriate to who you are. Don't get fancy merely for the sake of being fancy. And don't be intimidated by the creativity of others. Do it your way, remembering that words always will be the central mode of communication.

The Use of Humor

Humor is a great tool in communication. To have a wry view of ourselves is a good thing. But some people are better with humor than others. Know your gifts! And don't use humor to hide. Sometimes a joke deflects attention away from a crucial issue. The challenge is to interject notes of lightness at appropriate points in your tale.

How Long Will It Take?

The actual time it takes to write a spiritual autobiography will vary from person to person. The scope of the job depends partly on your age. The older you are, the more you have to report. It also depends on how long you have been conscious of the spiritual side of life.

I have known people who put together a spiritual autobiography in a matter of hours. I have known people for whom it took weeks of hard work. Do what you need to do, given the time and circumstances you are working with.

And remember, your spiritual autobiography is meant to be told, not read. Therefore, the most important thing is to prepare in such a way that the tale will be told well.

ISSUES IN PREPARING A SPIRITUAL AUTOBIOGRAPHY

Being Honest

It would be wonderful if our lives were filled with sweetness and light so we could describe what nice people we are and how our coming to God was simply a matter of learning how to meet God. Maybe this is your tale, but I suspect it isn't. In fact, your spiritual autobiography may not be a pretty story at all.

Many of us are better at running away from God than welcoming God. All of us are flawed and distorted to one degree or another. That's part of being human. We live on a fallen planet—fallen people living with other fallen people. In fact, our fallen state is what engages us in the search for God. We do not know God easily and directly. We are all like the prodigal son, who left his father's house to run his own life in a far country.[1] In each of our stories, there will be notes of darkness, betrayal, willful evil, lostness, sin. The story of our coming home to the Father is often a confused and bleak tale. To pretend that it is not is just that—to pretend.

This is not to say that everybody's story is about life among the swine (to continue with the prodigal son imagery). In fact, our "lostness" may be found in our "righteousness"—our attempts to be perfect people who always do the right thing (like the prodigal's elder brother). The truth of that kind of tale is often the hardest to discover because so much energy has gone into denial, hiding, and pretending we are good. It's important to remember that fallenness reveals itself in different ways in different people. But it is here, in our fallenness, that we begin to notice God's voice, so our sinfulness needs to be described to some extent.

What about the courage to tell our tale to others? Can we really be candid? Do we want to be candid? *Should* we be candid? These are not easy questions to answer. One thing is clear: we need to be brutally honest with ourselves. That is hard enough. We also need to be candid with at least one other person. When we tell our whole story, we gain power over what lies in the darkness. Darkness cannot stand the cleansing power of light, as the apostle John told us long ago.[2] Light diminishes the grip darkness has over us.

This is why you need to be as honest as possible when you share your spiritual autobiography with a small group. A group where confidentiality prevails and each person tells his or her tale honestly (no one is exempted from the process) is a potent force for change. When we tell our tale in all its ugliness (and with all its grace) and then find we are still loved, forgiven, and accepted, we find new life. When we know one another in this way, it brings deep connection and warm generosity. It is difficult to dislike those who have given you the gift of their stories.

But there are appropriate levels of honesty. The basic principle is this: do not share information that will hurt others. Beyond that, you need to consider the level of trust that exists within the group. Ideally, each group will grow in its ability to trust. Openness leads to more openness, so that you even can share what you have never shared before.

Dealing with Past Hurt
In writing a spiritual autobiography, you may uncover issues that cause you pain. When you locate an incident from the past that still pricks strong emotions in you, this is a sign that the situation has not yet been dealt with completely. In such a case, two things are important. First, don't become preoccupied with the painful incident. Don't give it more attention than it deserves. Remember that your primary task is writing a spiritual autobiography. Don't allow one incident to cloud your sense of the whole. Second, resolve to deal with this issue once your spiritual autobiography is written. Write out the incident in full detail in your journal. Make plans in your journal to get help. This may mean discussing the problem with a friend, writing letters of confession or confrontation, or seeing your pastor or a therapist. In other words, deal with the issue but not in the context of the spiritual autobiography.

Not Becoming Overwhelmed
The whole idea of producing a spiritual autobiography is so daunting to some people that they are tempted to stop before they start. "I can't do this!" they exclaim. "I can't write. I don't know enough about the spiritual side of life. I have nothing to say. I can't remember much about my past. And even if I could,

I'm not a good talker. I could never tell all this stuff to others."
This is fear. It is very real but it should be rejected. Look at
your own objections. Write them down on a piece of paper. (It
is important to identify fear specifically rather than leaving it
on a vague level that you cannot work with.) Now commit
these fears to God. Ask for God's guidance and strength in
beginning this project.

One of our fears is that we are being asked to write a book:
My Life from a Spiritual Point of View or something like that.
This is wrong. Our only task is to take about thirty minutes to
tell our story to others who are there to hear it.

Another fear is that doing this project will take a lot of
time, wisdom, and skill. In other words, this is something only
very gifted people (or full-time religious professionals) can do.
This is simply not the case. First, everyone has a story to tell.
No one is overlooked in the activity of God. Second, everyone
can tell his or her story. It does not need to be complex or
filled with wise insights. It does not have to cover every detail.
Simply talk about how you have related to (or run away from)
God. Pick a few important experiences and describe them:
your first communion, a profound answer to prayer, discovering that God actually knew and loved you. Tell the group
about your contact with church groups of various sorts: being
part of a religious fellowship at college, finding a church when
you moved into a new community, visiting a retreat center.
Describe your rebellion against God and the questions about
God that you wrestle with. Don't make this such a big deal
that you freeze up!

On the other hand, do as thorough a job as you can, given
the time and circumstances. Producing a spiritual autobiography means different things to different people at different
points in their lives. To some, this is a matter of life and death.
They must know where they are now and where they have been
in their lives. They will pursue that knowledge relentlessly
because it is the only way they can make sense out of their
lives. For others, this is a good exercise in getting to know one
another. Remember: do what you can and don't worry about
what you can't do. This is not something you do only once. You
can continue to work on this project after the group ends.

A Checklist for Writing a Spiritual Autobiography
Here is a brief summary of how to prepare and write your spiritual autobiography.

- ❏ Determine the date when you will present your spiritual autobiography.
- ❏ Organize your time so you will not be rushed at the end.
- ❏ Read pages 57-103 of this book, which describe the complete process of preparing a spiritual autobiography.
- ❏ Pray for God's guidance. Continue to pray and listen to God throughout the process.
- ❏ Divide your life into various periods of time (either by age-based or search-based periods; see pages 65-71).
- ❏ Explore each period (the places, people, and experiences of each age period; or the three periods of the search for God: Quest, Commitment, and Incorporation).
- ❏ Examine each period of time for the high points (encounters with God: mystical, conversion, charismatic, and daily experiences; see pages 71-72).
- ❏ Examine each period of time for the low points (crises of faith: doubt, disobedience, darkness, depression, circumstances; see pages 72-75).
- ❏ Look for the outcomes of growth (intellectual, emotional, behavioral, relational, growth in service; see pages 75-78).
- ❏ Describe each period in writing—either with notes or by writing a manuscript (see pages 79-80).
- ❏ Time yourself as you practice presenting your story.
- ❏ Delete as many sections as necessary to get your story down to the allocated time (see pages 81-82).
- ❏ Present your spiritual autobiography to your group.
- ❏ Continue to explore your spiritual autobiography on your own as a way of deepening your understanding of and growing in your spiritual life.
- ❏ Work on the discipline of noticing God (see pages 89-103).
- ❏ Tell parts of your story as often as possible and appropriate.
- ❏ Add to your story as time goes on.

Notes
1. Read the story of the prodigal son in Luke 15:11-32.
2. 1 John 1:5–2:2.

THE SPIRITUAL DISCIPLINE
OF NOTICING

The spiritual skill one learns in writing a spiritual autobiography is that of noticing. We learn to notice God's presence throughout our lives.

This is not a natural sensitivity for most people—though there are some who seem to have been born attuned to the supernatural. Most of us, however, need to develop a sensitivity to the spiritual. We need to become open to the many ways in which the Divine affects us. This is why I call this the discipline of noticing. It takes effort on our part to master this skill. A spiritual discipline is an activity that we practice so that it will become habitual for us and a normal part of who we are. The practice of spiritual disciplines is sometimes misunderstood to be a mark of piety. In fact, it is a sign of need. If we did it easily and naturally, then we would not have to practice the discipline![1]

The aim of the discipline of noticing is to move the spiritual from the edges of our lives to the center. God has created us to live within both the natural and the supernatural realms. But because of our brokenness, our natural habitat has become the world of sense and time. We barely notice the spiritual. Therefore, we have to work at recovering this lost sense of the Divine.

The problem, of course, is not that God is hiding and needs to be coaxed out into the open by our prayers and supplications. God is active in the world around us. God is willing to be in relationship with us. The problem is not with God. The problem is with us. We are unaware or barely aware of God's presence, so we must learn to notice.

A spiritual autobiography is a concrete way to notice God. In this chapter we will examine seven other ways by which we notice the presence and work of God. In some cases, the presence of God bursts upon us (as in a mystical experience). We cannot help but notice God. In other cases, we place ourselves in settings that allow us to notice God (such as Bible study and prayer). In all of these ways, we grow attuned to the supernatural (in the midst of the natural) and so we develop our spiritual lives.

THE SEVEN WAYS

Mystical Experience

Sometimes God bursts in on our lives in such a way that even the most indifferent among us cannot miss his presence. These are easy events to note as we write a spiritual autobiography. However, we need to be aware that mystical events can come in various ways.

Encounters with God: In certain instances, a person is confronted with the presence of the Divine in unmistakable ways. There is a sense of Presence. Sometimes there is a light, a voice, or a physical phenomenon. For example, on the Damascus road, a light greater than the Middle Eastern sun flashed around Paul and his companions. He heard a voice that revealed the essence and meaning of his life. His companions were struck to the ground and rendered speechless. There was a sense of Presence. Someone was there who knew Paul's name. This Presence turned out to be Jesus. In his dialogue with Jesus, Paul received a call that changed the rest of his life. Such experiences are unusual (though remarkably widespread—one research study indicates that more than thirty percent of adult Americans have had a mystical experience).[2]

Brushes with God: Not every experience of the Divine is so overwhelming. More common are what might be called mild mystical experiences. For example, in the course of reading the Bible, a text comes alive in an almost tangible way, and you know that God is speaking to you. Or while on vacation you sit in the garden of an old Spanish monastery, and you sense something about that place that rings of the Divine. Much prayer has been offered here. You rest in that reality for a long time before you move on to your next destination.

Longing for God: This is what C. S. Lewis calls "the inconsolable longing": for an instant, we are drawn away from this world into another world—a world where we find ourselves deeply at home. We discover that this is where we truly belong. But just as quickly as this comes upon us it vanishes, leaving behind a deep longing for what we encountered. We may return to the music, the words, or the place that triggered the experience, but we find only the longing. Lewis would argue that these are genuine intimations that our true home is with God and that someday, God willing, we will live there.

Empowerment by God: The New Testament tells us that we can expect the Holy Spirit to give spiritual gifts to us, such as hospitality, wisdom, healing, tongues, and teaching. The nature, character, and use of these gifts is the subject of other books. Suffice it to say that sometimes we encounter God through these gifts, as recipients (we are healed when someone lays her hands on us and prays) or as practitioners (in the classroom we sense that we are much better teachers than, in fact, we should be; it is as if God is guiding us). Through charismatic gifts we know God.

Relationship with God: God is alive and present for us. God is no mere concept, but a companion. We pray. We listen. There is dialogue. There is awareness.

These experiences change us. We lose our fear of death. We become more loving people. We find our true calling. We set aside lesser things that were once attractive to us. We develop a thirst for the spiritual. Mystical experiences have a prominent place in our spiritual autobiography. What mystical encounter have you had? What role has that experience had in your pilgrimage?

The Bible
I would like a world where the mystical was normal; where God touched me constantly and deeply so that my fear disappeared, my questions were answered, and I became a deeply spiritual person. But that, alas, is not the way God operates. Were this the norm, I suspect we would have little need for faith. We would simply "know." As it is, we have a sufficient record of God's interaction with our planet and the people on it. This is what lies at the core of the Bible: the revelation of

91

who God is, how we meet and know him, what reality is all about, and how to become what we were meant to be. "The entire Bible is a record of God's speaking in human history."[3] To understand and absorb the Bible (much less to live it out in our lives) is a long and demanding process. In fact, it takes a lifetime—and even then we will have hardly begun.

How do we notice God by means of Scripture? In the Bible we find:

The story of God: We learn of God's interaction with humanity. The many stories in Scripture alert us to God's presence in our lives. We learn what our lives mean. We know where to look for God. In particular, the story of Jesus gives a face to God. Jesus is what God looks like in time and space, living on our planet as a human being.

The wisdom of God: We learn how we are meant to live. We learn to see events through a biblical worldview. We gain insight into what is happening around us and how to respond.

The challenge of God: We find our calling from God, both our particular place in God's scheme of things and the way we should live daily.

The praise of God: We find hymns and prayers that have been used for centuries in expressing devotion to God in worship and thanksgiving.

The Bible opens to us the work and character of God. It helps us to see God. It enables us to distinguish between God and other realities. It trains us in the ways of God. What role has the Bible played in your pilgrimage?

Nature

God is the creator. This is God's planet and we are the people God has fashioned from the dust of the ground. Thus, our whole world bears the imprint of God. Of course, the trick is noticing God's handiwork. One way we do this is by way of metaphor. A metaphor displays an attribute of something else. With metaphor we move from what we see and know to what we do not see or know. For example, sitting in the midst of a vast, green meadow dotted with spreading maple trees, covered with delicate flowers, alive with bees and birds, we learn about God's beauty. "If God created this tranquil paradise, how much more beautiful and peaceful must God be. . . ."

A few years ago I visited Victoria Falls in Zimbabwe. It is such an improbable phenomenon. Upriver from the falls the mile-wide Zambizi River flows along at a leisurely pace. Then this quiet, steady, forceful African river suddenly confronts a great gash in the earth. It is as if someone took an ax and plunged it deep into the ground, cutting the river in two. The river, in protest and with great agitation, plunges over the edge and falls hundreds of feet to the canyon below. As it falls over the edge and dives down to the bottom, the water roars and boils. It sends up great clouds of mist and spray. It becomes a wild, enraged torrent before racing through the canyon below and over the cataracts, having been reduced from a body of water one mile wide to a swift and dangerous river a few hundred yards wide.

Standing there at the edge of Victoria Falls one cannot help feel the wild, untamed, irresistible power of God. As you peer through the mist, the falls are revealed, then suddenly concealed, only to be revealed again in a different way, much like the way in which God's power and presence are hidden and revealed in our lives, hidden only to come at us in a new way from a new place. I am not particularly sensitive to nature and what it tells us about God, but even I could not miss the sense of God's creative power at Victoria Falls.

We sometimes decry people who say, "nature is my church." We feel (rightly) that we need to meet with others on a regular basis to praise and worship God, rather than sit alone on a beautiful lake in the early morning. However, in saying this we may miss what is called "natural revelation." We can learn a lot about God by viewing creation with enlightened eyes. Again, the issue is learning to see properly. We must learn, for example, to distinguish between original creation and fallen creation. The earth and the people God created were perfect. But then a distorting element was introduced through human disobedience to God, and the world hasn't been the same since. A good creation was marred. We need to see beyond the flaws (hurricanes, disease) to the original (the grandeur of sea and mountain, flowers, giraffes). In what ways have you learned of God by noticing his creation?

Inner Experience

God speaks with a still, small voice within us—that is the testimony of many men and women down through history. How God speaks is the subject of conjecture (through our minds, the unconscious, in sub-audible ways); that God speaks is a matter of experience. God uses various means to convict us.

An inner sense of rightness: There is a tone, a sense that sometimes comes to us that carries its own weight of authority.

A divine compulsion (as opposed to a neurotic compulsion): This is a sense of the "ought."

An inner voice: When we pray we often receive new insight, we find wisdom to confront what we are struggling with, or we gain a sense of mission as we listen. If prayer is, indeed, a conversation and not a monologue, we need to learn to hear God's voice and to distinguish that voice from all other voices.

Dreams: The men and women of the Bible assumed that God could speak through dreams. For example, if Joseph had not known that God could speak through dreams, he would not have understood the nature of Mary's pregnancy, nor would he have known he should flee to Egypt with his wife and child to avoid Herod's wrath. Most dreams are not from God. Some are, however, and these generally have a sense of rightness about them.[4]

Dallas Willard would argue that the "gentle whisper" or interior voice "is the preferred or the highest form of individualized communication for God's purposes."[5] This is not so strange when we remember that Paul says, "We have the mind of Christ" (1 Corinthians 2:16).

The problem with inner experience, however, is that it is internal. There is no external validation to what we sense. The danger is that we may attribute to God what is not from God. On the one hand, we need to learn to recognize the voice of God by being in relationship with God. On the other hand, we should accept inner urgings with some care, testing them with Scripture (are they consistent with God's voice there?), with the church (does this fit in with tradition?), and with those to whom we are accountable (what do those who know us best say?).

What experiences of "hearing God" have you had in the course of your pilgrimage? How has this affected you? Changed you?

Worship and Contemplation

If God speaks to us in Scripture and prayer, then we should set aside time to engage in these practices, which are most conducive to noticing God. The rhythm of each person's conscious pursuit of God differs. For some, this involves a daily time set aside for Bible reading, prayer, reading religious texts, contemplation, and worship. For others, the focus is on public worship. Perhaps a weekly small group Bible study is the center of your conscious pursuit of God. Or it may be periodic visits to a retreat center or a spiritual director. The point is not what we do by way of devotional practices, but that we give ourselves some space in which we say, "Speak, for your servant is listening" (1 Samuel 3:10).

There is yet another way in which we hear God's words: through the voice of other people. Perhaps the most common experience of this comes in worship. A sermon is preached, and in some way it resonates with us. We understand in a new way; we are challenged to a new path; we grasp a new truth. It is clear in Scripture that God speaks through people. For example, God appointed Moses as his spokesman (Exodus 4). The prophets knew that they spoke the word of God (see, for instance, Jeremiah 20:9 and Micah 3:8). In a lesser way, there are times when we sense that we or others are saying something that has come from beyond us. The word of God "can and does come to us through the living personality, mind, and body of other human beings as they, in unison with God, speak to us."[6]

What role has worship (the community seeking God) and contemplation (the individual seeking God) played in your spiritual pilgrimage?

Relationships

In the parable of the sheep and goats, Jesus said,

> "Then the King will say to those on his right, 'Come, you who are blessed by my Father; take your inheritance, the kingdom prepared for you since the creation of the world. For I was hungry and you gave me something to eat, I was thirsty and you gave me something to drink, I was a stranger and you invited me in, I needed clothes and you clothed me, I was sick and you looked after me, I was in prison and you came to visit me.'
>
> "Then the righteous will answer him, 'Lord, when did we see you hungry and feed you, or thirsty and give you something to drink? When did we see you a stranger and invite you in, or needing clothes and clothe you? When did we see you sick or in prison and go to visit you?'
>
> "The King will reply, 'I tell you the truth, whatever you did for one of the least of these brothers of mine, you did for me.'" (Matthew 25:34-40)

Apparently, we meet God when we respond to others in need. This is, after all, what the Great Commandment is all about: "You shall love the Lord your God . . . and your neighbor as yourself" (Mark 12:30,31). To follow Christ is to be a member of this community of love where we meet God in one another. It is not that we are all divine or anything like that (God is God; human beings are made in the image of God). Rather, the Spirit of God works in and through people. We sense the presence of God's Spirit in loving acts of kindness. Through others we learn about who God is, how we are meant to live, and what community is all about. We are changed by these encounters. God has changed us.

What is the role of other people in your pilgrimage? I suspect that this will be a major area of concern in your spiritual autobiography. People affect our journey in all sorts of ways.

They start us thinking about faith: Who first raised religious questions for you? How? In what ways did they help you take the next steps in your faith pilgrimage?

They introduce us to Jesus: How did you come to follow Jesus? Who had the greatest impact upon you in this regard?

They model faith for us: Who are the wise men and women who guided and shaped your pilgrimage? How did they do it?

They care for us in times of need and celebrate with us in times of joy: Who in your community of faith has nurtured, supported, loved, and rejoiced with you over the years?

They open themselves to us for care and support: To whom have you reached out in the course of your pilgrimage? In what ways? With what results? How did you grow?

Your spiritual autobiography could not be written without including the names of many others. The Christian pilgrimage is not a solitary journey. It is a matter of walking alongside the Company of the Committed (to use Elton Trueblood's phrase). Our stories are intertwined with the stories of many others. In them we come to know about God and, in fact, to know God through them.

Fruit of the Spirit

Scripture reveals a concrete way to identify God's presence. In Galatians 5:22-23 Paul says, "the fruit of the Spirit is love, joy, peace, patience, kindness, goodness, faithfulness, gentleness and self-control." When we encounter any of these qualities, in some way we are in touch with the Spirit of God. As we notice these good fruits, we give thanks to God. Likewise, we should seek to display these attitudes in our lives. In this way, we yield ourselves to the work of the Spirit.

Think about times in your life where you have encountered these qualities. Then reflect on ways in which God was there.

Love. "God is love" (1 John 4:7-12). It not just that God brings love (God does), that God promotes love (God does), nor that God desires for us to be in loving relationships (God does). It is that God's essence *is* love. Thus, where love prevails, in some way God is there. In Greek there are four words that are translated "love." In the Galatians text the word used is *agape,* which refers to actively reaching out to others simply because they are in need and without regard to reward or response. This is the kind of love God inspires in us and others.

Joy is not the same as happiness. Rather, it refers to a deep inner attitude of delight. This joy is not disturbed by hardship. It is connected with hope, which knows there is an inheritance waiting for us in God's future.

Peace is not contentment as much as it is a deep contentedness. The root meaning of this word is not negative ("an absence of conflict"), but positive ("the presence of that which brings wholeness and well-being"). The presence that brings this peace is God.

Patience is the ability to persevere with people who aggravate or persecute you. It is the ability to bear up under stress. This is not a natural trait!

Kindness is an attitude toward people, a way of relating to others.

Goodness is closely related to kindness. It is, perhaps, a more active way to relate to others in word and deed.

Faithfulness is the character trait of reliability. A faithful person is someone you can depend on.

Gentleness is another character trait: the ability to defuse conflict or find creative ways through conflict.

Self-control is the ability to master the desire and compulsion for self-gratification.

The first four virtues (love, joy, peace, and, by implication, hope) find their root in God. To display these qualities is to be touched by God. When we encounter these virtues in other people, we encounter God's Spirit at work. The next three virtues (patience, kindness, goodness) are expressed in relationship to other people. They are signs of love in action. Again, as such, they give evidence of the work of the Spirit. The third set of virtues (faithfulness, gentleness, and self-control) are more personal. They describe human character as it ought to be and again mark the work of the Spirit. In your pilgrimage, who are the people who display these traits? How do you learn of God from them?

Each of these seven ways helps us to track God's presence. The story of that Presence is the essence of a spiritual autobiography.

ISSUES IN NOTICING GOD

Being Loved by God

Central to our experience of God is knowing that God loves us. The mystical writers have much to say about this (Bernard of Clairvaux, Evelyn Underhill, Julian of Norwich, Ignatius of Loyola). This knowledge, perhaps more than any other, gives focus to our lives. It is one thing to know theoretically that God loves us (because the Bible tells us so) and another to experience that love (in direct and concrete ways). All of the above experiences—mystical encounter, worship, fruit of the Spirit, and so on—communicate that God loves us, and communication is at the heart of a loving relationship. To open oneself to God's flame of love is the foundation upon which awareness of God rests.

The Dark Night of the Soul

Mystical writers speak of "the dark night of the soul." This is the experience of God's absence. These writers explain that this experience seems to come to people who are about to move from a kind of spiritual kindergarten to a deeper spirituality. They also say that this experience weans us away from wanting God's presence mainly for the spiritual thrill and security that it (rightly) gives us, to a state in which we simply want God. It is important to notice that the absence of God is felt only because it comes after we experience God's vivid presence. We cannot know what we are missing if we never had it in the first place. For most of us, however, the issue is that we do not know the presence of God, not that we have lost the sense of God's presence.

Lethargy

If it is true that God is constantly present, that God loves each of us individually—not just as a generalized group—and that God desires a conversational relationship with us, why do we not spend more time with God? Why is the development of a "devotional life" so hard for so many of us?

There is no single answer to this question. The issue may be a combination of several factors.

No sense of God's presence: We don't spend time with God because it all feels so impersonal. To read the Bible and pray seems like a duty, not a joy. These are pious good works that we are told will benefit us. The lack of a sense of presence may be a matter of never having sought a relationship with God. Or it may be a matter of not expecting God to be present or not knowing what the term "presence" really means.

No sense of relationship: We will relate to God, in some sense, the way we relate to other people. The ability to enter into comfortable relationships varies from person to person and results from factors such as early socialization, family dynamics, an introverted versus an extroverted personality type, opportunities for friendships, past rejection, and so on. If you can spend a whole day with your spouse and be content with routine and occasional conversation, little emotion, and no real interaction, then these dynamics will probably be at work as you relate to God.

No conversation: Our devotional life becomes a burden when we do all the thinking and all the talking. Bible study is reduced to learning; prayer, to making requests. There is no conversation; that is, there is no silence where we listen for God and are open to God. But when one's meditations include both speaking and hearing, there is a different quality to them.

No time: Time is doled out equally to all people. The issue is how we use it. This, in turn, is a matter of circumstance and need. Some have little free time because they must work long and hard to survive. Others have little time because they work hard in order to feel good about themselves. Still others fritter away time or give it to lesser pursuits. Seeking God takes time. This does not mean that we have to enter a monastery or convent to find the time, nor that we have to give up high-demand jobs to be spiritual. It does mean that we have to work at finding time.

We can find chunks of time if we look: commuting to and from work; engaging in routine chores that leave our minds free for other activities; rising a half-hour earlier or going to bed a half-hour later (if we are getting adequate sleep); shifting from an exercise bike to a long walk; the final twenty minutes of lunch break; and so on. We also can find time through the choices we make. We easily can watch television every night, but we must *choose* one evening away from the tube. We can read on a regular basis, but we must *choose* less leisure reading. I suspect that in the rush of contemporary life we will have to discover new ways of seizing time for our relationship with God. In fact, we may not find the time to sit and be with God. Rather, we may learn to speak with God while we are engaged in routine tasks.

No routine: Those who are strong "Js," to use a Myers-Briggs term (Js are people who need order, control, and routine) will struggle with knowing God unless they include God in their routine. Strong "Ps" (the more spontaneous types, such as Saint Francis was reputed to be) can seize the moment; Js have to schedule the moment.[7]

A Way to Begin Noticing

How do we begin the practice of noticing God? One way is by using the prayer of *examen*. This is a way of prayer developed by Saint Ignatius, originally for use by the Jesuits (the mission order he founded). Noticing God is one of the aims of this prayer. It helps develop in us a greater awareness and sensitivity to the concrete ways in which God has been working in our lives over the past day. The more acute our sense of God's work, the better we are able to respond to God. Using the prayer of *examen* is a concrete way to begin practicing the discipline of noticing.

The prayer of *examen* is a three-part prayer process.[8] First comes gratitude. We scan the previous twenty-four hours in order to notice the gifts God has given us. We thank God for all of this. Second, we review the previous day again, this time seeking to notice God's presence. We ask the Holy Spirit to show us in the everyday events of the past day where and how God has been present and working in us. Third, on the basis of our gratitude for the gifts of God and our awareness of his work, we again examine our day. This time we ask the Spirit to show us the ways in which we have failed to respond to God or not lived up to our calling as Christians. We ask to know our sin and failure. Because we come to sin and failure through the path of gratitude and awareness of God's presence, we are able to face and own these shortcomings; we know that even in the midst of them God still loves us and is at work in our lives. We don't make light of our shortcomings. On the contrary, the more we are aware of God's active love for us, the more sorrow we feel for our refusal to respond, and the more effort we make to follow God. But we do this out of gratitude, not guilt.

The discipline of noticing is not an isolated activity, unconnected with the rest of our spiritual life. It is part of that life. As we practice other spiritual disciplines (such as the disciplines of prayer, worship, study, meditation, service, and celebration, not to mention the discipline of spiritual autobiography), we learn the discipline of noticing. This is as it should be. A spiritual discipline is never an end in itself. It is a means to an end. That end is loving God and enjoying God forever.

Notes

1. See *The Spirit of the Disciplines* by Dallas Willard for a discussion of the nature of spiritual discipline.
2. There are numerous examples in the Bible of this sort of phenomenon: the fire from God, which passed through Abraham's sacrifice (Genesis 15/17); the call of Moses in the burning bush (Exodus 3:3-10); the call of Isaiah (Isaiah 6), and so on. In addition, there are many examples of people addressed by angels: Abraham in Genesis 18–19 (see also Hebrews 13:2, which says we may entertain angels without knowing it), Joshua (Joshua 5:13-15), Daniel (Daniel 9:20-27), Mary (Luke 1:26-38), and Peter (Acts 5:19-20).
3. Klaus Bockmuehl, *Listening to the God Who Speaks* (Colorado Springs, CO: Helmers & Howard, 1990), p. 13.
4. The Bible contains many examples of God speaking through dreams and visions: Abimelech (Genesis 20), Jacob (Genesis 28), Joseph (Genesis 37), Nebuchadnezzar (Daniel 4), Paul (Acts 16:9), and Peter (Acts 10:9-19).
5. Dallas Willard, *In Search of Guidance* (San Francisco: HarperCollins, 1993), p. 91.
6. Willard, p. 101.
7. For more information on the Myers-Briggs Type Indicator see David Keirsey and Marilyn Bates, *Please Understand Me: Character and Temperment Types* (Del Mar, CA: Prometheus/Nemesis Book company, 1989).
8. Though the prayer of *examen* is sometimes described as having five aspects or moments (gratitude, light, the account, deepening, and forearming), I have focused on what seem to be the three key movements.

A SELECT BIBLIOGRAPHY

Books About Spiritual Autobiography

Baldwin, Christina. *Life's Companion: Journal Writing as a Spiritual Quest*. New York: Bantam Books, 1990.

Keen, Sam, and Anne Valley-Fox. *Your Mythic Journey: Finding Meaning in Your Life Through Writing and Storytelling*. Los Angeles: Jeremy P. Tarcher, Inc., 1989.

McClendon, James W. *Biography as Theology: How Life Stories Can Remake Today's Theology*. Philadelphia: Trinity Press International, 1990.

Peace, Richard. *Pilgrimage: A Handbook on Christian Growth*. Grand Rapids, MI: Baker, 1976.

Shea, Daniel B. *Spiritual Autobiography in Early America*. Princeton, NJ: Princeton University Press, 1968.

Trent, John. *Life Mapping*. Colorado Springs, CO: Focus on the Family Publishing, 1994.

Wakefield, Dan. *The Story of Your Life: Writing a Spiritual Autobiography*. Boston: Beacon Press, 1990.

Weibe, Katie Funk. *Good Times with Old Times: How to Write Your Memoirs*. Scottdale, PA: Herald, 1979.

Spiritual Autobiographies: A Sample

Buechner, Frederick. *Sacred Journey: A Memoir of Early Years*. San Francisco: HarperCollins, 1982.

Colson, Charles. *Born Again*. Old Tappan, NJ: Chosen Books/Revell, 1976.

Griffin, Emilie. *Turning: Reflections on the Experience of Conversion*. New York: Harper & Row, 1984.

Jones, E. Stanley. *A Song of Ascents*. Nashville, TN: Abingdon, 1972.

Lee, D. John, ed. *Storying Ourselves: A Narrative Perspective on Christians in Psychology*. Grand Rapids, MI: Baker, 1993.

Lewis, C. S. *Surprised by Joy: The Shape of My Early Life*. New York: Harcourt Brace Jovanovich, 1956.

Merton, Thomas. *Seven Storey Mountain*. New York: Harcourt Brace Jovanovich, 1948.

Wakefield, Dan. *Returning: A Spiritual Journey*. New York: Penguin Books, 1988.

Weibe, Katie Funk. *Border Crossing: A Spiritual Journey*. Scottdale, PA: Herald, 1995.

Books About the Discipline of Noticing

Bockmuehl, Klaus. *Listening to the God Who Speaks: Reflections on God's Guidance from Scripture and the Lives of God's People*. Colorado Springs, CO: Helmers & Howard, Inc., 1990.

Edwards, Tilden. *Living in the Presence: Disciplines for the Spiritual Heart*. San Francisco: HarperSanFrancisco, 1987.

Huggett, Joyce. *Listening to God*. London: Hodder & Stoughton, 1986.

Johnson, Jan. *Listening to God: Using Scripture as a Path to God's Presence*. Colorado Springs, CO: NavPress, 1998.

Payne, Leanne. *Listening Prayer: Learning to Hear God's Voice and Keep a Prayer Journal*. Grand Rapids, MI: Baker Books, 1994.

Pytches, David. *Does God Speak Today?* Minneapolis: Bethany, 1989.

Willard, Dallas. *In Search of Guidance: Developing a Conversational Relationship with God*. San Francisco: HarperSanFrancisco, 1993.

LEADER'S NOTES FOR THIS STUDY

The Art of Leadership

It's not difficult to be a small group leader. All you need is:

❖ The willingness to lead
❖ The commitment to read through all of the material prior to each session
❖ The sensitivity to others that will allow you to guide the discussion without dominating it
❖ The willingness to be used by God as a group leader

It's also not hard to start a small group. All it takes is the willingness of one person to make some phone calls. Here are some basic small group principles that will help you do your job.

Ask the questions: Let group members respond.

Guide the discussion: Ask follow-up questions (or make comments) that draw others into the discussion and keep the discussion going. For example: "John, how would you answer the question?" or "Anybody else have any insights into this question?"

Start and stop on time: If you don't, people may be hesitant to come again since they never know when they will get home.

Stick to the time allotted to each section: There is always more that can be said in response to any question. It's your job to make sure the discussion keeps moving from question to question. Remember: it's better to cut off discussion when it's going well than to let it go on until it dies out.

Model answers to questions: Whenever you ask a question to which everyone is expected to respond (for example, a

"Telling Our Stories" question as opposed to a Bible study question), you, as leader, should be the first person to respond. In this way you model the right length—and appropriate level—of response.

Understand the intention of different kinds of questions:

❖ Experience questions: The aim is to cause people to recall past experiences and share these memories with the group. There are no right or wrong answers to these questions. They help group members share their stories and think about the topic.

❖ Forced-choice questions: Certain questions will be followed by a series of suggested answers. Generally, there is no "correct" answer. Options aid group members and guide their responses.

❖ Questions with multiple parts: Sometimes a question is asked and then various aspects of it are listed below. Ask the group members to answer each of the sub-questions. Their answers, taken together, will answer the initial question.

❖ Analysis questions: These force the group to notice what the Bible text says and to explore it for meaning.

❖ Application questions: These help the group make connections between the text and their lives.

Introduce each section: This may involve a brief overview of the focus, purpose, and topic of the new section and instructions on the exercise.

Guide the exercises: Details of how to lead each session follow this chapter. Be sure to read notes for the first meeting.

Comment: Occasionally bring into the discussion some useful information from your own study. Keep your comments brief. Don't allow yourself to become the "expert" to whom everyone turns for "the right answer."

The Structure of Each Session

There are five parts to each small group session. Each part has a different aim.

Stories: The purposes of this section are to help people move from the concerns they brought with them to the small group to the topic itself; to start people thinking about the topic in terms of their own experiences; to start discussion among group members; and to help people get to know each other by telling some of their stories.

Discuss: The purposes of this section are to discuss the process of preparing and presenting a spiritual autobiography; to develop clear expectations for each person; to motivate and encourage one another in preparation; and to plan together for the presentation of spiritual autobiographies.

Study: The purpose of this section is to study the Bible together. This involves a brief introduction to the text, reading the text, and working through the questions in order to understand what the text is saying and how it applies to each person.

Pray: The purposes of this section are to end the session with prayer related to the issues discussed and to commit the process of spiritual autobiography to God.

Homework: The purpose of this section is to guide group members in the preparation of a spiritual autobiography.

How to Lead Each Session

The small group leader follows this process in each of the five Bible study sessions.

Welcome

Open in prayer: Your prayer does not need to be long or complex. You can write it out beforehand. In your prayer, thank God for being present. Ask God to guide the group into new wisdom and to give each person the courage to respond to the text. If you like, you can ask others beforehand if they would be willing to do the opening prayer for a given session. (It's a good idea to ask beforehand, rather than putting someone on the spot.)

Introduce the topic: Take no more than a minute or two to do this. Simply refer to the three sections in the beginning of each chapter.

Preparation for Sharing: This describes the intention of the Discuss section, in which the group takes care of business in preparation for the autobiography sessions.

Bible Study Theme: This describes the focus of the text and its connection to the process of spiritual autobiography.

Session Aims: The goals of the session are summarized.

Stories

Read aloud the brief introduction (when there is one) or simply introduce the theme of the exercise.

Give people a minute to read over the questions and think about their answers. Then, as leader, begin the sharing by giving your answer to the first question. There are no "right" answers, only personal stories or preferences. Laughter is great medicine. These questions are seldom serious and invite funny stories. Move to the person on your right or left and ask him or her to respond. Go around the circle so that each person has a chance to respond to the question.

Move to question 2 and do the same. Finish with question 3. You can skip question 3 if you run out of time. But watch the time carefully so that everyone has a chance to respond. After a few sessions you will know how many questions you can get through with your group. You may need to pre-select one or two questions to use for sharing time.

Remember that even though this is lighthearted sharing, you are discussing the topic of the Bible study. Remind people of the theme.

Discuss

Identify the issue or issues of that session's discussion.

If there is a reference to material in this book, ask people to turn to it and read it over quickly.

If there are tasks to be performed (such as developing a schedule for sharing spiritual autobiographies), be sure to complete them.

Be encouraging as you discuss the joys and trials of preparing a spiritual autobiography.

Keep in mind that the essence of this small group is sharing spiritual autobiographies. This is why you are meeting. Use this time to prepare for that.

Study

Introduce the Bible passage by reading aloud (or summarizing in your own words) the introduction to this section.

Read the Bible passage (or invite someone else to read it).

Give the group a few minutes to read over the passage, read through the questions (and think about the answers), and consult the Bible Study Notes.

Ask the first question; get responses from several people.

When you feel that the question has been sufficiently discussed, move to the next one.

In this section, some of the initial questions are fact-oriented. There are specific answers to them. Subsequent questions will be more open-ended and will invite discussion. Spend only a little time on the fact questions. They encourage people to notice carefully what the text says, but the heart of the study is found in the discussion related to the meaning and the application of the text. If you spend too much time on fact questions, the Bible study can become boring. Keep up the pace. Feel free to omit some of the fact questions if time is a problem.

Notice that each question set begins with a title that defines the focus of that set of questions. The title helps you understand the direction of the questions. Sometimes you may want to ask only one question under a given title.

Work through all of the questions, skipping some sub-questions as time permits. Be sure you have thought about the questions beforehand so that you recognize the important questions that need more time.

If you have time, use the optional question. These quotations invite discussion and personal sharing that will fill the remaining time. You may decide to skip some questions and end with the optional question.

Remember: your aim in the Bible study is to help the group understand better the nature of a spiritual pilgrimage so that they have insight into their own pilgrimage and will find it easier to write their spiritual autobiographies.

Conclude

End with prayer together. The topics of prayer are defined. Develop a style of prayer that fits your group. This may be:

Free prayer: people pray about the topics as they feel led.

Conversational prayer: one person begins praying about a topic in a sentence or two, then a second person joins the conversation and prays a few more sentences, and so on until a person begins to pray about the next topic.

Liturgical prayer: give people time to write down a short prayer that they will read during the prayer time.

Leader prayer: the leader or someone who has volunteered prays for the whole group.

Silent prayer: after the allotted time, the leader closes with a brief spoken prayer.

Discuss the Homework for the coming week. Encourage people in their work on their spiritual autobiographies.

Hospitality
Serve hot and/or cold drinks, and perhaps also some dessert food. Food and drink give people a chance to talk informally. There is often good conversation after a small group session as people hash over the discussion.

Adapting Material for Your Group
There are three ways to conduct this small group program.

Full Option: Follow the program as outlined in the book, that is,

❖ Do the five Bible studies on the pilgrimage of Abraham and cover the various organizational details. During these five weeks, group members will work on their own to prepare their spiritual autobiography. This will involve reading pages 57-103 of this guide individually and then writing their spiritual autobiographies (five weeks).

❖ Follow the Bible studies with as many small group sessions as necessary for each person in the group to present his or her spir-

itual autobiography (five to thirteen weeks).

❖ Conclude with the Celebration described on pages 53-56 (one week).

Shortened Option I: Follow the Full Option, but skip Bible study sessions 4 and 5. This option saves two weeks.

Shortened Option II: Skip all of the Bible studies and go straight to the presentation of spiritual autobiographies. However, you will need at least two organizational meetings before the first person presents a spiritual autobiography. These two meetings are necessary for the group to get to know one another (it is hard to present an honest spiritual autobiography to a group of strangers) and to create a good structure within which to present the stories.

❖ Week one: Use the Stories ("Biographies"), Discuss (how to write a spiritual autobiography), and Pray sections from small group session 1. In addition, do the Discuss section in session 2 (creating a covenant). Make sure you have a volunteer who will present his or her spiritual autobiography in week 3.

❖ Week two: Use the Stories and Pray sections from session 2 ("Family Stories"), the Discuss section from session 3 (sharing a spiritual autobiography and making a calendar for sharing), and the Discuss section from session 5 (starting spiritual autobiography sessions).

❖ Week three: and following: For each subsequent week, allow one person to present his or her spiritual autobiography. If you are really pressed for time, you can expand these sessions to two hours and do two spiritual autobiographies per session. However, experience shows that the best sessions are limited to one person per week. You may or may not want to do the final Celebration session. However, if you skip that session, spend some time deciding what the small group will do next at the end of the final spiritual autobiography (see "What's Next" on page 55).

Session 1: Pilgrimage

The first session is crucial. People will be deciding whether they want to be a part of the group. So your aim as leader is to:

❖ create excitement about this small group (so each person will want to continue),

❖ give people an overview of the series (so they know where they are headed),

❖ build relationships (so that a sense of community starts to develop), and

❖ encourage people to commit to the small group (so everyone will return next week, and perhaps bring a friend!).

Potluck

A good way to launch the first session of any small group is by eating together before the session. Sharing a meal draws people together and breaks down barriers between them.

Ask everyone to bring along one dish for the supper. This makes it easy to have a meal for twelve! Or if you feel ambitious, you might want to invite everyone to dinner at your place. What you serve doesn't need to be elaborate. Conversation (not feasting) is the intention of the get-together.

The aim of the meal is to get to know one another in this informal setting. Structure the meal in such a way that a lot of conversation takes place.

After the meal, be sure to complete the first session, not just talk about what you are going to do when the group starts. People need to experience what it will mean to be a part of this small group.

Introduction to the Session

Welcome: Greet people and let them know you're glad they've come and you look forward to being with them for the next few weeks.

Prayer: Pray briefly, thanking God for this group and asking him to guide your deliberations and sharing today. Ask God to guide you in discovering the power of a spiritual autobiography to teach you the discipline of noticing God's presence.

Group process: Describe how the small group will function and what it will study. Discuss, specifically:

Series theme: The aim is to prepare and present a spiritual autobiography.

Group Experience: Describe how the five Bible studies will function, and then how each spiritual autobiography will be presented and discussed.

Group details: Discuss where you will meet, when, and how long each session will last.

Group goal: Spiritual growth through writing and presenting a spiritual autobiography, and through learning the spiritual discipline of noticing God, is the goal.

As you begin session 1, use "The Structure of Each Session" on page 107 as a guide. Be alert to the following issues:

Stories: This session's purpose is to build relationships by sharing brief stories and information. The theme of the exercise is "Biographies" and is

110

intended to provoke thinking about spiritual autobiography. Don't let question 3 take much time. When you (as leader) answer this question, do so in a few sentences as a model for the others. Remember that this issue will be covered thoroughly as you each present your spiritual autobiographies.

Discuss: Don't spend a lot of time reading the material on preparing a spiritual autobiography. Just glance at it. This material should be read individually between group sessions. The aim of this discussion is to encourage people to think about writing their spiritual autobiography.

Study: Keep in mind constantly that the aim of this Bible study (and those that follow) is to expand each member's understanding of spiritual pilgrimage and to make it easier to write a spiritual autobiography. Keep this focus during each session.

In general terms, the first two sets of questions focus on the Hebrews 11–12 text, while the last two sets of questions focus on the application of the material to each person's life.

Question 2 is an example of a fact-oriented question that should be answered quickly. Notice that the themes of movement and goal in pilgrimage are emphasized.

Try the optional question. This invites more of an unstructured discussion. If it works well with your group, you may want to leave time in each of the following sessions for this exercise.

Group invitation: If your first session is a "trial meeting," invite everyone to return next week. If you have room in the small group (for example, there are less than twelve people), encourage members to invite their friends. After week two, new people cannot join the group because each time a new person comes it is necessary to rebuild the sense of community.

Session 2: Call & Blessing

Introduction to the session: Welcome new people and let them know you're glad that they have come and that you look forward to your time together. As you did last week, open in prayer and quickly explain the aims of the session.

Do session 2. Use "The Structure of Each Session" (page 107) as a guide. Be alert to the following issues:

Discuss: A clear covenant is important because it gives group members confidence that what they share will be well received and kept within the group.

Study: Continue to distinguish between questions that need little time to answer and those that invite reflection and discussion.

Session 3: Encounters

Do session 3. Use "The Structure of Each Session" (page 107) as a guide. Be alert to the following issue:

Study: This is a longer passage than you have studied together so far. You may want to ask the group to read it silently, since this will be quicker. Also, no one will have to pronounce the names in verses 19-21!

Session 4: Relationships

Do session 4. Use "The Structure of Each Session" (page 107) as a guide. Be alert to the following issues:

Discuss: The issue here will be to encourage one another in the writing process. Some people may be having difficulties.

Study: Now you have two passages to work through, not one. You will have to be careful not to spend too much time on one passage. Give each equal weight. Keep the focus in mind as you guide the discussion. Be sure to get to question 9. This will generate good discussion, especially because the group has been thinking about these things as they write their spiritual autobiog-raphies.

Session 5: Testing

Do session 5. Use "The Structure of Each Session" (page 107) as a guide. Be alert to the following issues:

Discuss: Get ready for the first spiritual autobiography session next week. Take whatever time you need so that session 6 will run smoothly.

Bible Study Notes: Because this is a difficult passage to understand, some background information is included on page 48. Make sure that the group reads these notes before thinking about the study questions.

Session 6: Presenting an Autobiography

You have now come to the reason this group is meeting: to hear each other's spiritual autobiographies. It is important that the session leader do everything possible to facilitate a good session. Be clear about who does what, and watch the time carefully.

Final Session: Celebration!

It is important to bring closure to every small group, and especially to one like this that has shared deeply with one another.

112